The Management Toolbox
55 Really Useful Management Tools

The Management Toolbox
55 Really Useful Management Tools

Teik P Oh

Queensbury Publishing
2016

Copyright © 2016 by Teik Peng Oh

www.teikoh.com

All rights reserved. This book or any portion thereof may not be reproduced or used in any manner whatsoever without the express written permission of the publisher except for the use of brief quotations in a book review or scholarly journal.

First Printing: 2016

ISBN 978-1-326-52496-8

Queensbury Publishing
P O Box 4157
Wembley WA 6913

Contents

About the Author 1
Introduction 3
Over-arching Management Tools 4
    The Problem-Solving Model 5
    Six Thinking Hats 10
    LACE 14
    SMART 17
Analysing Issues 20
    Brainstorming 21
    Nominal Group Technique 23
    Mind Mapping 25
    Flowchart 28
    Check Sheet 30
    Benchmarking 32
    Run Chart 34
    Market Segmentation 36
    Break-even Analysis 38
    Employee Engagement Survey 41
    PESTLE 43
    SWOT Analysis 45
    Pareto Chart 47
    Pie Chart 49
    Urgent/Important Matrix 51
    Teamwork Index 54
    Stratification 61
    Cause & Effect Diagram 63
    Five Why's 66
    Scatter Diagram 68

Venn Diagram 70
Product Features and Benefits Analysis 72
Customer Value Matrix 74

Developing Solutions 76
The Pareto Principle 77
Decision Tree 78
The Product Development Process 82
Customer Attractiveness Matrix 88
Affinity Diagram 91
Crossover Analysis 94
Training Matrix 97
Management Presentation 99
Business Model Canvas 101
Quality Circles 103
Organisation Charts 105
Job Descriptions 107
Policies and Procedures 109
Force Field Analysis 112
Vision and Mission Statements 115
Strategic Planning 118
Business Planning 121
Scenario Analysis 124
Action Planning 126
Critical Path Analysis 128
Sales Component Analysis 130
Five P's of Marketing 133

Implementing and Measuring 135
Change Management Process 136
Negotiating Using Interests not Positions 138
Risk Management Analysis 146
Experiential Transfer Process 151
Ratio Analysis 154
The Balanced Scorecard 158

Tools in Alphabetical Order 161
Tools by Task 163

Teik P Oh

About the Author

Teik P Oh is the founder of successful consulting company OTS Management, creator of the business coaching blog Teik Oh Dot Com, and an independent Director on various commercial and Not-for-Profit company Boards, as well as a frequent speaker at management meetings throughout Australia.

Teik qualified as a Chartered Accountant in England in 1982 and had a high-flying career with international financial services and consulting companies in four continents before he settled in Australia and created OTS Management, a consulting company with a vision to provide international consulting experience to Australian small businesses and Not-for-Profit entities. Teik is widely recognised throughout Indigenous Northern Australia as a provider of valuable management consulting services to Australian Indigenous businesses and NGO's, including successful Native Title Prescribed Bodies Corporate. He also services mainstream small businesses in various industries throughout Australia, helping them formulate strategy, develop markets, and grow profits through strategic planning, business planning, organisational change, and team development.

Teik's popular business development blog – **Teik Oh Dot Com: Strategy, Leadership, Growth** – can be found at *www.teikoh.com*

The Management Toolbox

Teik P Oh

Introduction

This Management Toolbox is a collection of the most useful management tools that managers will need to identify issues, define problems, gather potential solutions, choose the best solution, make decisions, implement initiatives, and measure success.

It is designed and laid out in such a way that, like a handyman's toolbox, you can reach into it at different times to find the right tool for the right job.

Use of the tools in the Management Toolbox avoids managers having to reinvent the wheel from scratch, when there are tools and models already out there that can be used to solve the problem or deal with an issue. When you are faced with a problem or issue, when you need to make a decision or are wondering "how do I..." you can reach into the toolbox and find a tool or model that you can use immediately.

While the tools are laid out following the "flow" of business management - identify the issues, seek solutions, decide on the best solution, design the introduction of the solution, implement the solution, and monitor the effects - the tables at the end of the book also cross-reference the tools against the tasks that manager's need to undertake. Using the tables, you can decide on the task you need to work on, find the best tools to help you with the task, and then pull them out and work with them on the task at hand.

The Management Toolbox

Over-arching Management Tools

While this Management Toolbox will provide problem-specific or task-specific tools for managers, there are a set of tools that could be applied throughout the problem solving process.

This set of tools represent an overview of management method - how to approach a problem, how to think effectively, how to communicate, and how to assess what you have done.

The Problem-Solving Model

When you need a process to solve a problem, starting from identification to implementation of a solution.

Managers have to solve problems on a day to day basis.

While there may be many different valid ways to enter into a process to solve problems, having a standardised problem-solving model allows you to address business problems in a systematic and structured way. A standardised problem-solving model ensures that you look at, process, and deal with all problems, whether technical, managerial or issues-based, in a consistent manner. The process removes personal bias and individualism, it makes problem solving easier and more effective by ensuring that you don't have to backtrack. Ultimately you can make your decision based on factual data gathered during the process rather than "best guess".

This is the six step problem solving model:-

The Management Toolbox

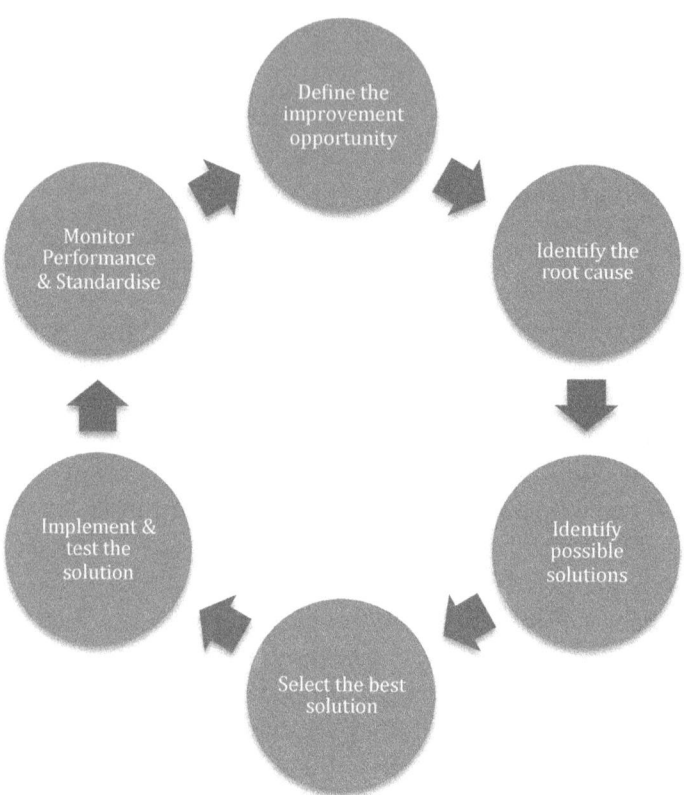

The Problem Solving Model

The process is circular; representing the fact that problem-solving is not a linear process and is often a continuous loop to ensure that "problems" are monitored.

Step 1 is to define the improvement opportunity. Stating it this way aligns your team gathered to solve the issue in a positive mind-set.

Problems can seem insurmountable; however viewing it as an improvement opportunity allows some free-thinking about what can be done. So, instead of asking "why do we always lose money launching new products?" ask instead "how can we improve product-launches to delight customers and increase sales?"

In this step you identify what can be improved. In doing so you need to write down exactly what the issue is, what the symptoms and effects are, and what may have caused it.

To define the improvement opportunity you can use some of the management tools in this toolbox on analysing issues such as brainstorming, check sheets and others.

Step 2 is to identify the root cause.

Some of the tools from this toolbox that an help you do this are the Cause & Effect Diagram (page 63), Five Why's (page 66), Pareto Chart (page 47), and Mind Mapping (page 25), amongst others.

In step 2, having defined the improvement opportunity, you collect information about the issue, organise the information to test out different possible causes, and then identify the root cause.

This will allow you to restate the definition of the improvement opportunity focused on the root cause so that the next steps concentrate on the root cause.

Step 3 is to identify possible solutions.

Until you investigate or test solutions, it is unlikely you will hit upon the ideal solution to fix the root cause. Even if you do, it may be a simple gut reaction to the problem rather than a real long term

The Management Toolbox

solution. In order to be creative you need to gather as many potential solutions as possible so that you can test them in relation to the root cause and possibly merge or improve alternative solutions.

Step 4 is to select the best solution. You should assess each potential solution for their effectiveness against the root cause and assess their strengths, weaknesses, opportunities and threats. You then choose the best solution based on effectiveness, strengths, technical feasibility, practical feasibility, affordability, and acceptability within the business.

Step 5 is to implement and test the solution.

Having chosen the solution you now need to plan for the implementation. This will involve the what, who, when and how questions - what must be done, what is required, who should do it, when must it be done by, and how will it be done.

This step also involves testing the solution implemented. Once installed, is it doing what it was intended to do?

Step 6 is to monitor performance and standardise.

In this step you monitor the performance of the solution over time. You would have tested that it "works" in step 5, but over time you will get to see some longer term effects - while it may be doing what it was intended to do, has the solution caused any side-effects, can its performance be improved with "tweaks"?

Once the results of the monitoring are in and assessed, the process can be standardised by writing new procedures or installing new systems.

Tips on how to use the Problem-Solving Model:

- Do not over-analyse – avoid paralysis by analysis

- If using it in a group situation, use Brainstorming (page 21) to generate discussion within each step of the model

Six Thinking Hats

When you need to ensure that everyone stays on track and collaborates effectively.

Six Thinking Hats is a method of structured thinking created by Edward de Bono, recognised as the father of lateral thinking. He wrote the book "*Six Thinking Hats*" which managers should read as a foundation work on clear thinking. The explanation here is intentionally brief and readers of this book should refer to de Bono's Six Thinking Hats for a more thorough explanation of the methodology.

The Six Thinking Hats methodology provides for managers to think effectively by planning their thinking processes in a structured, detailed, and cohesive manner.

In the book de Bono identifies six distinct paths in which the brain can be trained to think, and links a different coloured hat to each. Each of these six paths brings to the forefront of the conscious thought a particular aspect of the issue being considered. In deliberately planning the sequence of the six different paths of thinking to suit the matter being considered, the premise is that you can reveal the different aspects in the right order so that you can arrive at the right solution for that particular issue. As you use one hat at a time, discussion has to stay in the thinking path being represented - and only that path - until the discussion is exhausted and the next hat is put on.

The six hats are:-

- Blue - Thinking. Process control - What is the issue? What is involved? What is the goal? Summaries, decisions, conclusions?

- White - Facts. What hard data or information do we have? What more do we need to gather? What do we actually know?

- Red - Feelings. Emotional response - How do people feel about it? People can put forward their emotional response without justification.

- Yellow - Benefits. Logical identification of benefits - What are the benefits? What's positive about this?

- Black - Caution. Critical but logical judgment, what's wrong with this?

- Green - Creative. What new ideas? People can put forward new ideas without judgment from others.

A sequence may run something like this:-

1. Blue hat - outline what we are trying to do, what is the issue or problem.

2. Red hat - how to people feel about the problem?

3. White hat - gather information about the issue.

The Management Toolbox

4. Blue hat - analyse the information logically and identify causes and options.

5. Green hat - what could we do?

6. Black hat - criticise the options from a factual position, not emotional.

7. Yellow hat - identify the logical benefits of the options.

8. Blue hat – based on pros and cons and information, what's the best option?

9. Red hat – how do people feel about what is proposed?

10. Blue hat - decisions and plans

Each hat in the sequence should only be used for a few minutes, the quick pace aiding the thinking process so people are not allowed to "drift" into other modes of thinking. The red hat is often kept on for an extremely short period so that it reflects a real gut reaction and doesn't turn into a judgmental step. Care should be taken in the use of the black hat to ensure that it is a logical criticism of the idea, and not simply a statement of dislike.

A group using the Six Thinking Hats tends to be more collaborative because it is focused on one specific approach at a time and avoids circumstances where one person is reacting emotionally while another is trying to find benefits. The pace and "rules" also encourage collaboration where people don't criticise someone's new idea as it is presented, but have to wait for the right hat to be worn.

Tips on how to apply Six Thinking Hats:

- Read Edward de Bono's book!

- Make sure the team understands how it applies and they keep to the aspect represented by the hat being worn at the time

- Encourage people stating what hat they are wearing in discussions, especially if the discussion is unstructured and you can then formally suggest adopting the Six Thinking hats

- Before a discussion about a topic, agree on the sequence the hats should be used, in order to avoid jumping around

The Management Toolbox

LACE

When you need to communicate effectively.

LACE is an acronym for:-

- Listen actively
- Acknowledge
- Check for understanding
- Explore

It is a communication model that bases effective communication on seeking to understand first before you are yourself understood.

The model relies on two or more parties all exercising, in turns, the steps of the LACE model in the correct sequence. The steps are:-

1. Listen actively – when the other party speaks, concentrate on what they are saying; do not be or act distracted, for example writing your notes or looking out the window; do not think of your response as they speak – simply listen to hear the whole message including any physical and emotional cues.

2. Acknowledge – this step shows the person you are listening to, that you have listened, so that they feel engaged and so

that they in turn will listen to you. You can acknowledge by simply nodding, or through verbal cues such as "uh huh" and "mmm" at specific points which also have the benefit of registering those critical points in your memory.

3. Check for understanding – this step summarises what you have understood and acknowledged in the first two steps and proactively ensures all parties are on the same page. You can do this be repeating or paraphrasing key elements of their message such as "so, if I understand you, it is your opinion that we should....is that right?" Checking makes sure you understand and allows them to correct any misconceptions. You can, at this stage take notes of the confirmed points.

4. Explore – finally you can explore the contents of their message and ask for more information, put forward "what if" type questions, and see if their message can be added to or re-emphasised. This step is not necessarily to challenge (although that does come into it if you disagree as this sometimes represents your "turn" to provide your message) but rather to explore.

With practice, the sequence can take a matter of minutes or even seconds in steps 1 and 2 and the whole sequence can be iterative until all parties understand each other. However the sequence within the LACE steps is important – as you can see it could lead to conflict if in the middle of the Listen stage you start to interrupt and Explore.

Tips on the use of LACE:

- Ensure everyone in the team knows what LACE means and how to use it

- In the initial stages when everyone is unused to the model, verbally state what step you are following

- Be consistent, practice

SMART

When you need to assess something you have written such as goals, definitions or plans.

SMART is an acronym for:-

- Specific

- Measurable

- Achievable

- Result-oriented

- Timed

It is a tool that you can use as a guide to assess how effective your written statements are. These written statements may be vision statements, instructions, action plans, goals, objectives, strategies as well as many others.

You assess the written statement by asking if the statement is:-

- Specific enough? Is it worded in such a way as to avoid confusion and stands to be understood even by others who were not part of its drafting?

The Management Toolbox

- Measurable? Most written statements need to be measurable in order to check whether they have been achieved. For example an instruction to "change the assembly operation to be more productive" is not measurable whereas to "change the assembly operation to increase production by 20% in a given week" is.

- Achievable? This is a common-sense check to see that the statement is actually achievable. This does not rule out challenging targets but does look to identify unrealistic targets. What is unrealistic or unachievable may be a matter of opinion, but through tools such as Brainstorming (page 21) or Nominal Group Technique (page 23), you can get to an educated opinion.

- Result-oriented? The statement should be written in a way that focuses on the outcome rather than the process. For example a goal to "prepare a marketing plan" is about the process of writing a plan whereas a goal to "increase sales by…" is about the result of the process.

- Timed? Most written statements are about end-results whether a vision or a goal. Therefore these statements need to recognise a time when the end will be achieved. This establishes when something has to be done by and therefore helps in prioritising time and resources, as well as serves as a measure of achievement.

Tips on using SMART:

- Be consistent in its use

- Involve people not working on drafting the statements to assess it using SMART

The Management Toolbox

Analysing Issues

This collection of management tools is used to analyse issues and problems before solutions or decisions are formulated and implemented.

The management tools in this section can be used when working in teams and groups, especially in workshops and meetings, for information-gathering, in prioritising issues, and in the analysis of situations.

Brainstorming

When you need to expand your thinking to include all the dimensions of a problem (or solution) and create as many ideas as possible.

The term "brainstorming" has fallen into general use to loosely mean collective free thinking. As a management tool, brainstorming has a more formal application, whether used in a structured or unstructured way, to expand thinking around a singular issue, and limiting the time of each session so as to avoid increasingly irrelevant ideas.

Brainstorming can be used in two ways:-

1. Structured – In this method every person in a group must give an idea as their turn arises in the rotation or pass until the next round. No idea is considered "bad" (If you use Six Thinking Hats (page 10), this would be a Green Hat phase). This forces even shy people to participate but can also create a certain kind of pressure to contribute so has to be facilitated sensitively.

2. Unstructured – In this method, group members simply give ideas as they come to mind. It tends to create a more relaxed atmosphere but also risks domination by the more vocal members of the group.

Tips on Brainstorming:

- Everyone agrees on the question or issue being brainstormed – write it down on a flip chart or whiteboard so everyone can refer to it during the session to keep themselves on track;

- Never criticise ideas;

- Write on a flip chart or whiteboard *every* idea. Having the words visible to everyone at the same time avoids misunderstanding and reminds others of new ideas that may come from what is already written;

- Record the words of the speaker – do not edit or interpret; and

- Conduct each brainstorming session quickly – 5 to 15 minutes work well. In a workshop there may be a whole series of 5 to 5 to 15 minute brainstorming sessions on different questions or issues as they occur.

Nominal Group Technique

When you need to give everyone an equal voice in problem selection.

When selecting or prioritising problems to work on, it is often the case that the loudest or most authoritative voice sets the agenda. This can lead to lack of buy-in when working on a problem. Nominal Group Technique or NGT provides a way in which everyone has an equal voice.

The Nominal Group Technique process is:-

1. Have everyone in the team call out the problem they feel is the most important and write it on a flip chart or whiteboard.

2. Check that the same problem hasn't been written twice (even in different words) and combine any that need to be combined – but be sensitive if people feel they warrant separate treatment.

3. Write a letter of the alphabet next to each problem on the chart or whiteboard. For example if there are five problems, they are listed as A, B, C, D, and E respectively.

4. Ask each team member to rank A to E in order of importance where "5" is the most important and "1" is the least important. They may not repeat numbers and if they

The Management Toolbox

feel two problems are of equal importance they must choose which is more important.

5. Ask each team member to call out their scores and write the scores next to the problem. The chart or whiteboard may end up looking like this:-

   A   2,5,2,4,1

   B   1,4,5,5,5

   C   4,1,3,3,4

   D   5,2,1,1,2

   E   3,3,4,2,3

6. Add the scores of each problem. In the above example A scores 14, B scores 20, C scores 15, D scores 11, and E scores 15, so the most important problem is B and should be worked on first.

Tips on using NGT:-

- Make sure figures of authority agree to the approach, understand the value of buy-in

Mind Mapping

When you need to organise and classify information and show the relationship between different aspects of a situation.

A mind map is a pictorial representation of information and how the different aspects of the information relate to each other.

Here is an example of a mind map:-

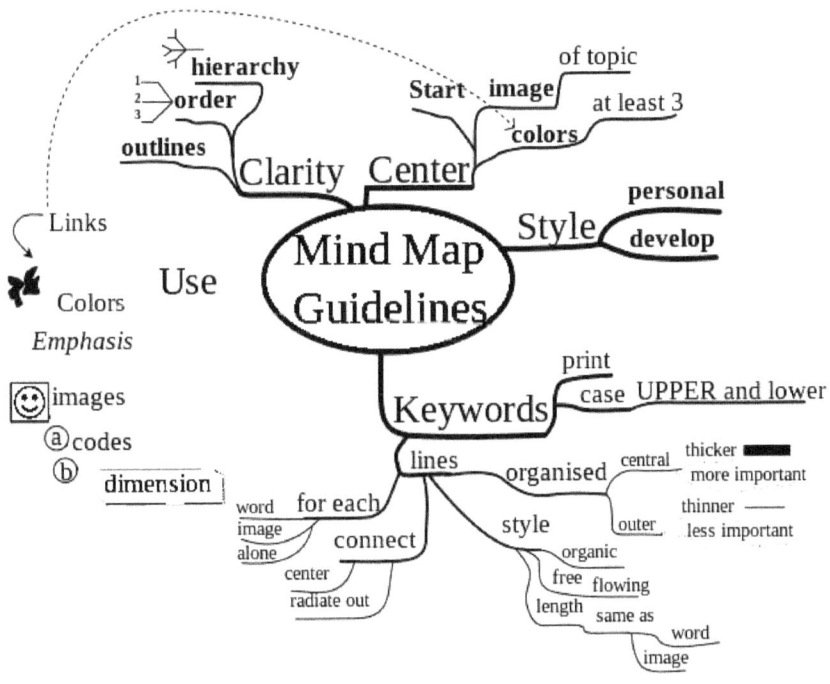

The Management Toolbox

A mind map starts with an idea, concept, problem, situation or issue, drawn in the centre. Associated ideas or effects caused by the central idea branches out from the centre, and other ideas branch out from them. By focusing on key ideas in your own words, then looking for branches and connections between ideas, you map the information in such a way as to help you understand and remember the information.

Mind maps can be used in analysis by visualizing the full extent of the issue or problem. They can structure and classify ideas, organise information, clarify structures of processes, and generate creative ideas around issues and problems.

To learn more go to www.buzan.com.au

Tips on creating mind maps:-

1. Start with the central idea in the middle;

2. Generate ideas or other concepts that result from the central idea;

3. Look for relationships – use lines, colours, arrows, branches to show connections between the ideas you generate. These relationships and their distinctive representation help you understand and remember the concepts generated;

4. Draw quickly without pausing, judging or editing – you can do this later but for the moment you do not want to revert to linear thinking;

5. Write down key ideas and move on – use upper case for emphasis, lower case to add notes.

The Management Toolbox

Flowchart

When you need to identify the actual and ideal path that any process, product or service follows in order to understand problems and identify deviations.

A Flowchart is a pictorial representation showing all the steps of a process. Flowcharts provide excellent documentation of a program and can be a useful tool for examining how various steps in a process are related to each other.

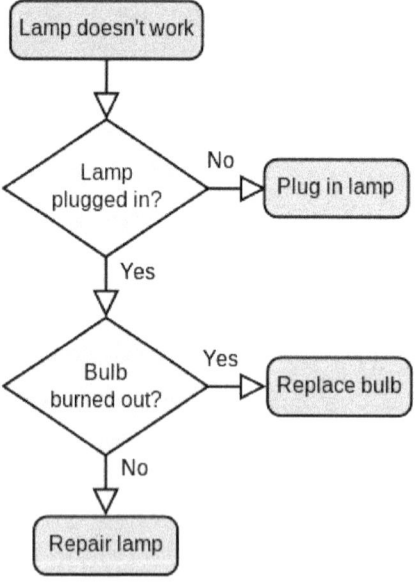

28

Flowcharts use easily recognisable symbols to represent the type of process performed, where the start and termination are clearly labeled, decisions are diamonds, and processes are squares.

By studying Flowcharts you can often uncover loopholes which are potential sources of trouble. Flowcharts can be applied to anything from Procedures Manuals to the journey of an invoice, the flow of materials, to the steps of making a sale or servicing a product or the steps to diagnose a problem.

Flowcharts can be used to correct an ineffective or inefficient process by drawing what steps the process actually follows, then drawing the ideal process eliminating waste and inefficiency.

Tips on the construction of Flowcharts:

- Define the boundaries of the process clearly – where is the start, where is the termination;

- Use the simplest symbols possible;

- Make sure every feedback loop has an escape;

- There is usually only one output arrow out of a process box, otherwise it may require a decision diamond.

Check Sheet

When you need to gather data based on a sample of observations in order to begin to detect patterns.

Check Sheets are an easy to understand form used to answer the question "how often does this happen?" Their use in recording observations begins the process of translating opinions into facts.

An example of a check sheet looks like this:-

Problem	Month			
	Jan.	Feb.	Mar.	Total
A	1,1	1,1	1	5
B	1	1	1	3
C	1,1,1,1,1	1,1	1,1,1,1,1	12
Total	8	8	7	20

Constructing a Check Sheet involves the following steps:-

1. Agree what event is being observed so that everyone is looking for exactly the same thing;

2. Decide on the time period to be observed, whether hours, days, weeks or months depending on what is appropriate;

3. Design a form that is clear and easy to use making sure all the labels are clear and there is plenty of space to enter data;

4. Collect data honestly and consistently, from a uniform point of view and ensure people have enough time to collect data seriously.

Tips for the construction and interpretation of Check Sheets:

- Make sure that the samples, observations and period are as representative as possible;

- Make sure the sampling process is easy and efficient so that people have time to do it and can do it easily;

- In constructing a Check Sheet the population being sampled must be homogenous (same machine, same person, etc.) and if not the population must first be stratified (grouped).

Benchmarking

When you need to compare your processes and performance to industry standard or the competition.

Your organisation's performance can be compared to others in order to assess how well you fare in the competition. Common metrics benchmarked are quality (e.g. number of rejects), time and efficiency, productivity, and financial benchmarks such as profitability. Anything that can be measured and that have comparable metrics can be benchmarked. Benchmarks are compared to industry standards, "best practice" in the industry, and the competition.

Typically the benchmarking process involves:-

1. Identifying the area or process to be benchmarked (usually a problem area or an under-performing area);

2. Understand how the current area or process works (using flowcharts(page 28), Check Sheets (page 30) and other tools);

3. Identify industry averages for the process or area from industry associations and studies;

4. Identify organisations that are leaders in these areas;

5. Survey target companies confidentially;

6. Analyse gaps and identify solutions;

7. Implement changes.

Tips on conducting Benchmarking:

- Obtaining comparison information is probably the most difficult process however there may be many sources of information available – official statistics, annual reports, industry bodies, university studies, Tax Office statistics, etc.

- Where the process you are investigating is unique to your situation (frankly, a rare occurrence) you can revert to past situations when it "worked well" or a realistic set of measures that you agree to be desirable and achievable.

Run Chart

When you need to show a simple display of trends.

Run Charts are the simplest tool to construct and use. Points are plotted on a graph in the order in which they become available over time. They can be used to graph machine downtime in minutes/hours, yield, errors or productivity as they occur over time.

An example of a Run Chart using observed number of defects from a process might be:-

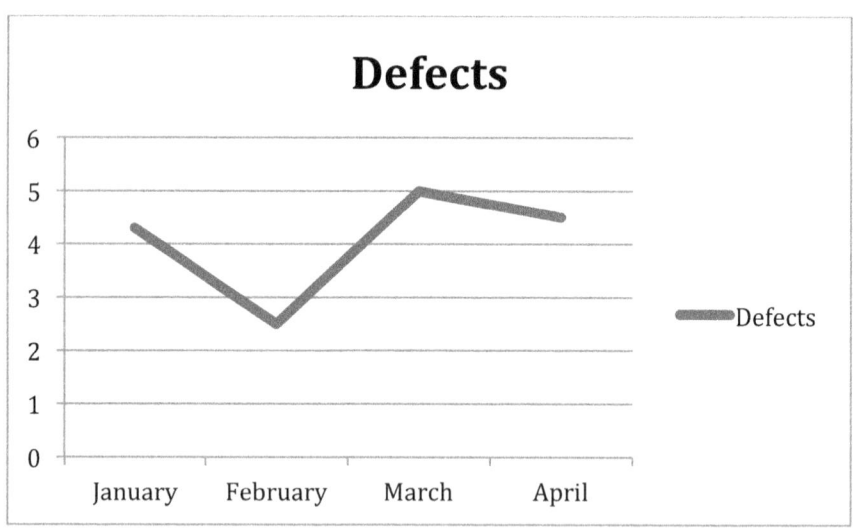

Tips on the interpretation of Run Charts:

- Be careful of the danger of seeing every variation as important – an understanding of the effect of any external factors is required;

- Use Run Charts to compare against average. For example when observing a process over a sufficient length of time it is to be expected that an equal number of points should be above the line of average as the points below. Therefore if a significant number of points are either above or below the average this indicates a statistically significant event and that the average has changed. Such changes should be investigated and if favourable, made permanent, if unfavourable, eliminated.

Market Segmentation

When you need to understand the different markets you serve, so that you can tailor activity to suit their requirements.

Market segmentation is arguably the most basic tool in marketing management. It is a critical tool in target marketing, so that you match your marketing efforts to that part of the market who have needs for your product.

Segmenting your market allows you to analyse them to select the best customers for your business, and then to enable your business to target its efforts on the most promising opportunities and attract them. Instead of scattering your marketing efforts, segmenting your market allows you to focus on the segment that represents the best return of marketing investment.

Your "Target Market" is that market segment or segments that are most likely to buy from you because their common characteristics show that they have needs your product can meet and they are likely to want those needs satisfied.

You can segment your market by organising them into segments with common characteristics. These can be:-

- Geographic;

- Demographic (age, sex, educational attainment, jobs, income, etc.);

- Psychographic (Lifestyle, design choices, early adopters, value perception, etc.); and

- Buying behaviour (loyalty, usage rates, habitual purchasing, price consciousness, etc.).

Tips on Market Segmentation:

- Start by identifying your homogenous market, the largest group of customers who are your market, whether your products appeal to "everyone" or to a large group such as "women" or "adults" or "drivers";

- Characterise the segments within your larger homogenous market by any or a combination of their geographic, demographic, psychographic or behavioural characteristics;

- Assess the identified market segments – how large is the segment, how easy is it to reach them, how much competition in that segment, will the segment grow or decrease?

- Use this knowledge to identify target market(s).

- To find out more read *"SMART Marketing – 7 Easy Steps to More Sales"* by Teik Oh (available from Amazon and the Apple iBook store).

Break-even Analysis

When you want to know how many units of sales of your product or service you need to sell in order to break even.

The break-even point is the point at which your sales revenue equals the total cost of your business (purchases, production costs, overheads, salaries). At this point you make neither a net profit nor a net loss i.e. a "break-even."

The break-even point is usually expressed as the number of units sold. Selling less than that number of units will result in a loss, and any more will result in a profit.

Break-even analysis can be used to:-

- Calculate the break-even point of your business or of one product;

- Help decide between buying different machines (which one has the lower break-even point);

- Help decide if you should introduce or discontinue a product (because the number you have to sell to break even is unachievable in the market); or

- Calculate the minimum selling price of a product, or your minimum total sales revenue required.

To calculate the number of units at break-even point, you use the formula:-

$$\frac{\text{Fixed Costs}}{\text{Selling price per unit} - \text{Variable cost per unit}} = \text{Break-even Point}$$

For example, let's say you want to calculate how much your minimum sales should be for your legal firm. Let's say the cost structure is:-

Annual fixed costs:-
Fixed salaries of lawyers   1,000,000
Office overheads including rent   500,000

Total Fixed Costs $1,500,000

Variable Costs:-
Sub-contract Lawyers $200 per hour
Selling Price:-
Fees charged at $500 per hour

Break-even annual hours required to be charged:-

$$\frac{1,500,000}{500 - 200} = 5,000 \text{ Hours}$$

Therefore break-even annual sales required is 5,000 Hours x $500 per hour or $2,500,000.

A Break-Even Chart for this example will look like this:-

The Management Toolbox

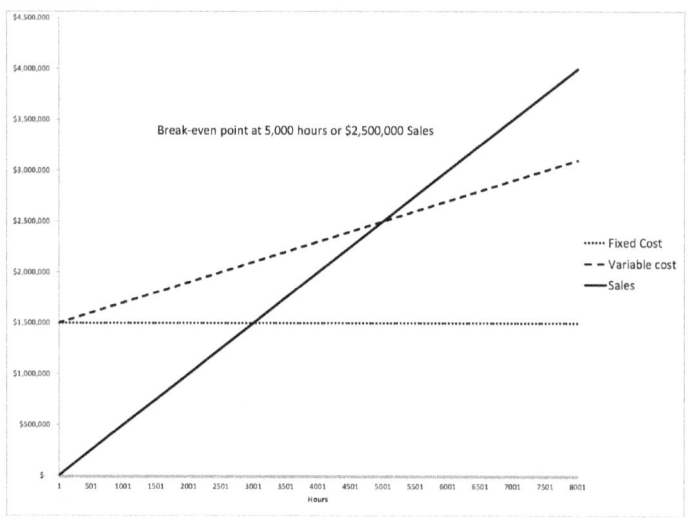

Tips on using Beak-even Analysis:

- Once you identify your break-even point, you can change different variables to see if you can increase profitability;

- Treat the analysis with common sense – there may be advantages between different choices that are not reflected in costs, and decisions about adding or discontinuing products may have further-reaching costs not in the analysis such as costs for additional training or costs of redundancy.

Employee Engagement Survey

When you need to gauge the commitment of your employees to the organisation.

An employee engagement survey measures how engaged employees are with their organisation. It does not measure happiness or job satisfaction. It measures emotive aspects of commitment such as pride about where they work, belief in the Vision and Mission of the organisation, and the perceived value their employers place on them and their contributions.

Employee engagement has been shown to drive revenue, customer service, and product quality. An employee engagement survey can highlight the "health" of employee input into those three outcomes and serve as an early warning of poor results to come.

Employee engagement surveys can be carried out annually and measure trend, or on demand at times of change, or on demand to give a narrower snapshot of that time, department, or issue.

Tips on carrying out an Employee Engagement Survey:

- Get a professional survey firm with experience in measuring employee engagement – do not attempt to draft your own questions;

The Management Toolbox

- There are several online Employee Engagement Survey systems that can conduct the survey and prepare reports of the results.

PESTLE

When you need to ascertain what external influences may affect your organisation in the medium to longer term.

PESTLE is an acronym for:-

- Political – local, national or global political policies, global issues such as war, which may have an affect on your business and markets

- Economic – Economic performance of the local, regional or national area, global issues, the stock markets, tax, interest, business confidence, need to be considered

- Societal – changes in lifestyle and buying trends, media, major social events that may impact on your business

- Technological – change in technology, innovation, communications occurring globally that may have an affect on your business

- Legislative – Local or national legislation and regulations and their effect

- Environmental – environmental issues whether local or global and their effect on the business

It is a tool to examine external factors that might have an effect on your organisation. Because these factors are examined from a macro point of view about macro-environment factors that could affect the position of your business and the growth or decline of the general market, the resulting potential factors tend to be more medium and long term factors. PESTLE is a useful tool when strategic planning as part of the answer to the question "where are we now?" It is also useful when analysing the feasibility of a major new project, amongst other uses.

Examining each category in turn, you list the trends and changes that are occurring externally. The results are then examined for the level of impact on the organisation and strategies are formulated accordingly.

Tips on using PESTLE:

- Keep the discussion at a macro level, talking about the wider environment, avoid narrowing into micro-changes to the PESTLE factors;

- Relate the results to the organisation – imagine the change taking place and how you would have to react. For example if there is likely to be continued international political tension, how will that affect your overseas markets?

SWOT Analysis

When you want to understand how a business, idea, process, product or project stands.

SWOT is an acronym for:-

- Strengths
- Weaknesses
- Opportunities and
- Threats

Strengths and Weaknesses are internal factors – those that the organisation has, to some degree, control over. Opportunities and Threats are external factors – the organisation does not control them, but can nevertheless be affected by them. It is traditionally used in strategic or business planning but can be used in any circumstance where a situation has to be analysed and its consequences understood.

The process involves first defining that which is being analysed. This may be the organisation, a part of the organisation such as a branch, a product or service, a process, a project, an idea, or even an individual.

The Management Toolbox

Once the object of the analysis is identified, you list all the Strengths and Weaknesses of the object; and you list all the Opportunities and Threats faced by the object.

The aim is then to reinforce and use the strengths, eliminate weaknesses, investigate opportunities and mitigate against threats.

Tips for using SWOT:

- Take each category in turn; as much as it is tempting, do not attempt to think of factors and then slot them into the appropriate category;

- After identifying strengths, weaknesses, opportunities and threats, take each identified factor in turn and identify the effect they may have to the situation;

- Identify some strategy or action against each strength, weakness, opportunity or threat – in planning, not all of these will make the cut but they are important raw ideas.

Pareto Chart

When you need to prioritise between issues.

A Pareto Chart is useful when you need to show the relative importance of all the problems or issues or conditions in order to choose the starting point. It is a special form of vertical bar graph, which helps to determine which problems to solve, and in what order. Doing a Pareto Chart based on tools such as Check Sheets (page 30) or other forms of data collection directs our attention and efforts to the truly important problems. You will generally gain more by working on the tallest bar than tackling the smaller bars.

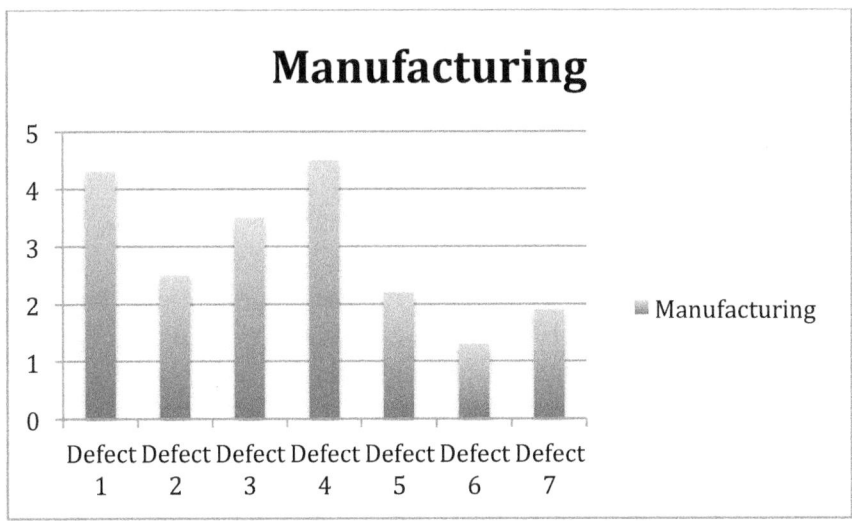

The Management Toolbox

In the above example, tackling the causes of Defects 4, 1 and 3 in that order should account for significant gains.

You can use Pareto Charts before and after a change to see what the effect of the change is.

You can also choose the highest bar, and then create a Pareto Chart for the components of that bar to find root causes. For example if you choose Defect 4 from the above example which represents incorrect welding, you may be able to do a Pareto Chart on welding machines, individual welders, welding shifts, and so on.

Tips on the use and interpretation of Pareto Charts:

- The most frequent problems are not necessarily the most costly nor necessarily the cheapest to fix – consider Pareto Charts on frequency as well as cost for a more complete picture;

- If clear differences do not emerge, regroup the data, by machine, by process, and so on;

- Use common sense – one customer complaint may be more important than 100 other complaints depending on the customer and what the complaint is about.

Pie Chart

When you need to show the proportions that make up a whole.

A Pie Chart is simply a graph represented within a circle, where the entire circle represents 100% but is broken into components making up that 100%.

Its use is similar to a Pareto Chart (page 47) and can be used to show the relative importance of different components of the problem or issue, however sometimes it can demonstrate the issue more clearly because it not only shows the *relative* frequency of the observed, but also shows how it makes up the whole.

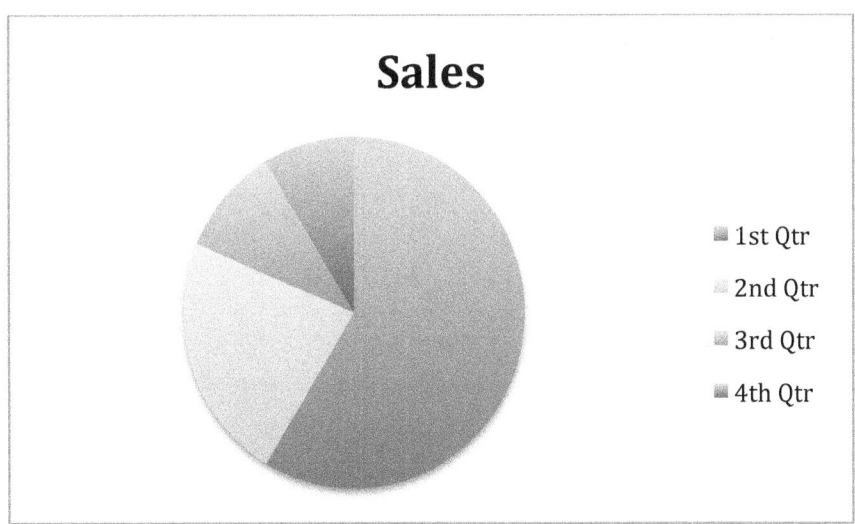

The Management Toolbox

Tips on preparing a Pie Chart:

- They can be prepared using software like Microsoft Excel;

- Use different colours for each component;

- Clearly mark the subject matter, titles of the components, the percentages within the pie if it makes it clearer to those who are more numerate than graphic.

Urgent/Important Matrix

When you need to categorise tasks or issues in order to prioritise them.

In his book *The 7 Habits of Highly Effective People*, Stephen Covey created a decision matrix to help people decide between what is important and not important, and what is urgent and not urgent.

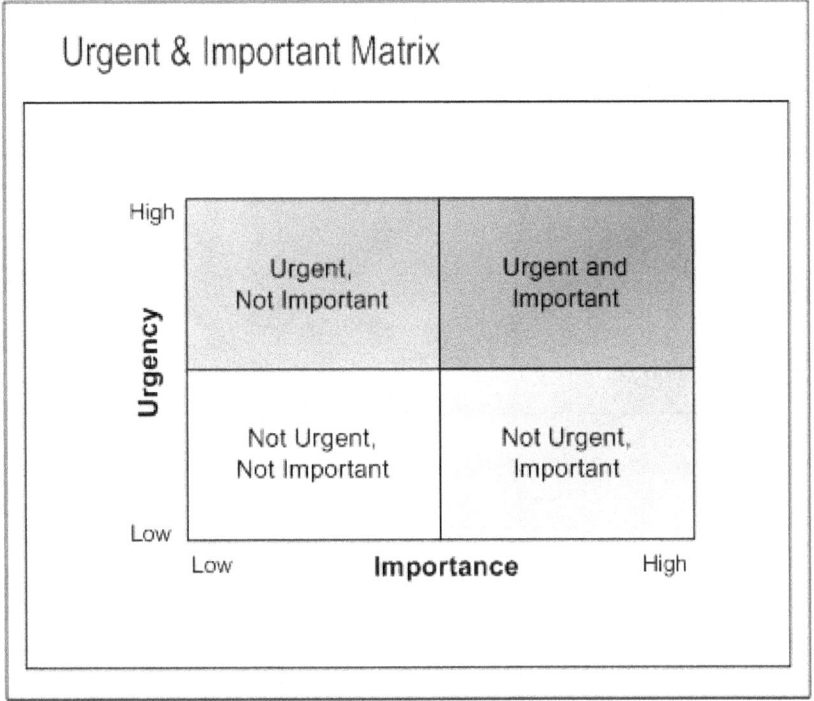

The Management Toolbox

Most of us fall into the trap that says urgent things are important and this matrix allows us to re-focus on what is really important.

The matrix is made up of an X-axis (horizontal) showing the level of Importance rising from left to right, a Y-axis (vertical) showing the level of Urgency rising from bottom to top. The measurement of importance and urgency may be on a scale of 1 to 10.

To use the matrix, you list the tasks or issues that you want to prioritise, then rank them in order of urgency and importance on a scale of 1 to 10. Your table of rankings may look like this:-

Problem	Importance	Urgency
Defect 1	1	3
Defect 2	4	10
Defect 3	9	9
Defect 4	9	4
Defect 5	7	10

The issues are then plotted into the matrix.

The top right quarter is deemed Important and Urgent. Those tasks should be done first due to both their importance and their urgency.

The bottom right quarter is deemed Important but Not Urgent. These are tasks that will have a significant effect on longer-term goals.

These tasks are to be scheduled so that resources are available to work on them properly.

The top left quarter is Urgent, but not Important. You should delegate these tasks.

The bottom left corner are tasks that are neither Important nor Urgent – avoid them or ignore them if you can, otherwise spend the least amount of time and resources on them.

Tips on constructing and using the Urgent/Important Matrix:

- Avoid a middle score like 5 in a scale of 1 to 10 – if you have to, award a half point so that it is 4.5 or 5.5;

- Keep clear the distinction between urgency and importance – some matters may be someone else's urgent matter that now impinges on you, and this does not necessarily make them important;

- In the longer term, you should be spending most of your time on the tasks in the Important but not Urgent quadrant so that you can work on longer term goals.

Teamwork Index

When you need to assess your team's ability to work as an effective team.

There are many Teamwork Indices available to assess the effectiveness of the team. These are a series of questions that team members answer individually, and the total responses are collated into an index of team effectiveness.

The following is one method of team assessment, based on the acronym "PERFORM" signifying the seven characteristics of a high-performing team:-

- Purpose – high-performing teams have a strong sense of shared purpose

- Empowerment – high-performing team members feel empowered to make decisions individually and collectively

- Relationships and Communication – high-performing teams maintain open and honest relationships and communicate effectively

- Flexibility – high-performing teams can adapt and are not necessarily bound by structures

- Optimal Performance – high-performing teams display strong task-accomplishment and results

- Recognition and Appreciation – high-performing teams independently maintain feelings of self-recognition of their achievements and express appreciation for each other

- Morale – high-performing teams maintain high morale even in difficult times

To calculate the teamwork index, first define the team and the context in which it works. For example, "this is the client-service team in the context of its relationship with clients."

Then, in each category below, circle **one** letter next to the statement that is most characteristic of your chosen group in context at this time. Be sure to think about the behaviours of the group as unit and not just the individual behaviours of the members.

Purpose

A   Members seem confused or disagree about the purpose and goals of the group and individuals' responsibilities. There is a discrepancy between the members' initial hopes and the reality of the situation in terms of what is workable and realistic.

B   Not all members have felt comfortable in expressing their views, and it is not clear if team members share a sense of common purpose. Members are more focused on "How do I fit in?" and "How will we work together?" Energy centres on defining goals, roles and tasks.

C   A sense of shared purpose is beginning to emerge. Goals for the team and individual roles are becoming clear, and the group is beginning to develop methods for achieving them.

D   Each member can describe and is committed to the purpose of the team. Goals and individual roles are clear and relevant to the overall purpose.

The Management Toolbox

There is a sense of interdependence and strategies for achieving goals are clear.

Empowerment

A Members feel cautiously optimistic about the ability of the group to solve problems and to achieve desired results. There is a growing sense of power as skills continue to deepen. The group is learning to work together to help each other.

B There is low confidence in the team's ability to realise a shared vision. Members are frustrated with leadership, policies, and practices. There is a sense of competition rather than collaboration among team members.

C Members feel relatively enthusiastic about the future of the team but have not yet acquired all of the necessary knowledge and skills. Policies, procedures and practices are unclear.

D Members feel a collective sense of power and have acquired the necessary skills and resources. Policies, procedures, and practices support the team objectives. There is a sense of mutual respect and willingness to help each other.

Relationships and Communication

A Team members are increasingly encouraging and supportive of one another. In doing so, they tend to withhold negative feedback. Members are listening to one another more and more.

B Team members express themselves openly and honestly without fear of rejection. Members listen to each other and express warmth, understanding, and acceptance. Differences of opinion and perspective are valued.

C Members often interrupt, withdraw, or express negative reactions to the formal leadership and / or each other. Communication within the group is guarded or volatile, reflecting conflict and / or frustration. The group shows little evidence of listening and understanding.

D   Members act politely and cautiously toward each other, reflecting a lack of knowledge of one another. Members look to the designated leader to moderate discussion. Members are often hesitant to express their feelings and opinions.

Flexibility

A   The team depends on the designated leader or formal structure for direction and approval. Members are cautious, formal, and / or stilted in their contributions to the group.

B   Frustration and tension in the group tends to limit the flexibility of members. Dissatisfaction is often expressed by "either / or" behaviour: aggression / withdrawal, dependence / resistance.

C   Members are beginning to share responsibility for team functioning by using the different strengths of the members. There is an emphasis on maintaining harmony and good working relationships.

D   Members share responsibility for team leadership and flexibly fulfil various roles for task accomplishment and team operation. Members freely express opinions and feelings and are adaptable to changing demands.

Optimal Performance

A   The team shows evidence of moderate to high task accomplishment. Team members are fairly agreeable in solving problems and making decisions.

B   The team accomplishes work quickly and effectively. Members have highly developed problem-solving and decision-making skills and value each other's differences in opinion and perspective.

The Management Toolbox

C　　The team shows little evidence of task accomplishment. Problem-solving and decision-making skills of the team are undeveloped.

D　　The team shows some evidence of task accomplishment. Members struggle with problem solving and decision making.

Recognition and Appreciation

A　　The team looks to the designated leader for recognition and appreciation. Members look to the leader for approval, more than to other team members.

B　　There is a strong feeling of respect and appreciation among team members. Individual and team accomplishments are frequently recognised by team members, as well as by the team leader.

C　　Team members rarely give recognition or express appreciation for each other. They tend to criticise each other or focus on the negative aspects.

D　　Team members increasingly express recognition and appreciation for one another, reflecting a developing sense of harmony and trust. This team spirit is somewhat tentative or fragile.

Morale

A　　Team members feel a sense of pride and excitement in being a part of the team. Their confidence is strong, and they are very satisfied with the work that is being accomplished.

B　　Team members feel a growing sense of team cohesion and confidence as they are learning to work together. Negative feelings are being replaced by positive ones.

C　　Team members feel a sense of expectancy and mild excitement, as well as some apprehension, as they anticipate working together.

D   There are feelings of frustration, pessimism, and dissatisfaction among team members. The team is fractured as members compete or psychologically drop out.

In order to calculate your Teamwork index, record the choices you made above by circling the letters you chose in the table below and write down the number of letters circled in each column. Multiply the number circled in each column by the number shown on the next line and write the result in the final line.

P	B	A	C	D
E	C	B	A	D
R	D	C	A	B
F	A	B	C	D
O	C	D	A	B
R	A	C	D	B
M	C	D	B	A
Number circled =				
Multiply Number circled by	1	2	3	4
Scores =				

Add all the scores to arrive at your Index (the total should be in the range of 7 to 28).

The higher the Index, the more characteristics of a high-performing team is displayed by your team.

The Management Toolbox

Tips on using the Teamwork Index:-

- The Index provides an indication of the effectiveness of your team based on the PERFORM acronym – review your Index to see what areas can be improved within the characteristics of PERFORM.

- A team may perform differently in different contexts. For example a sales team may be high performing in its relationship with customers, but perform poorly in the context of relationships with other internal departments. Ensure you clearly define which context people should have in mind when asked to assess their choices.

- The Teamwork index is best used when all the members of the team complete the questions so that a more complete and meaningful average score can be calculated.

Stratification

When you need to analyse data to find improvement opportunities.

Stratification helps analyse cases where the data actually masks the facts. This often happens when recorded data is from many sources but is treated as one number. For example, data for injuries in a mine may be recorded as a single figure, either rising or falling. But that sum may actually be the sum of total injuries, several types of which are falling but one of which is rising significantly.

Stratification breaks down single totals into *meaningful* categories or classifications to focus corrective action.

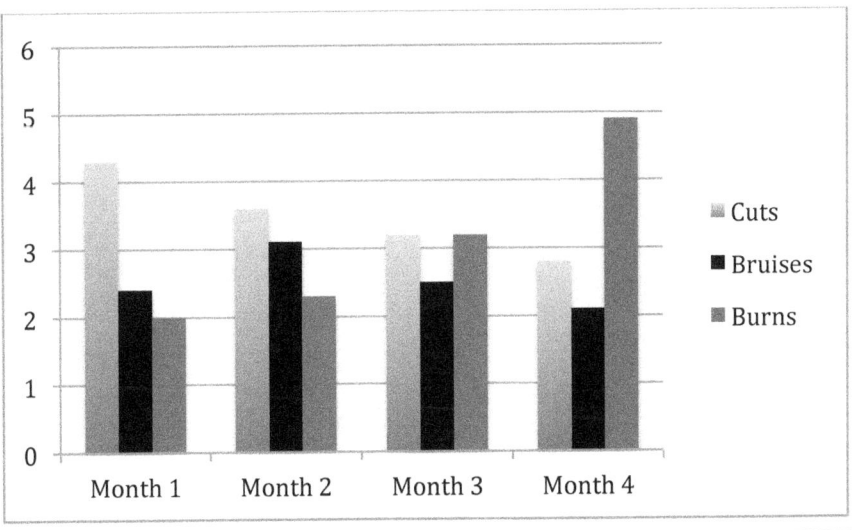

In the above example, stratification of minor injuries shows us that the incidences of cuts are falling, that the incidences of bruises are steady, but the incidences of burns are rising. Without stratification the reports of total injuries would have appeared reasonably stable at between 8 to 10 incidents per month.

Tips on using and constructing Stratification graphs:

- The aim of data-based problem solving is not to gather more data but to gather *meaningful* data, which means that some common sense needs to be applied before, and after data collection;

- Data to be compared must be gathered consistently;

- Don't over-complicate graphs.

Teik P Oh

Cause & Effect Diagram

When you need to identify, explore, and show the possible causes of a specific problem or condition.

These are sometimes known as "Ishikawa Fishbone Diagrams" named after the man who created them and the fact that they look like a fishbone.

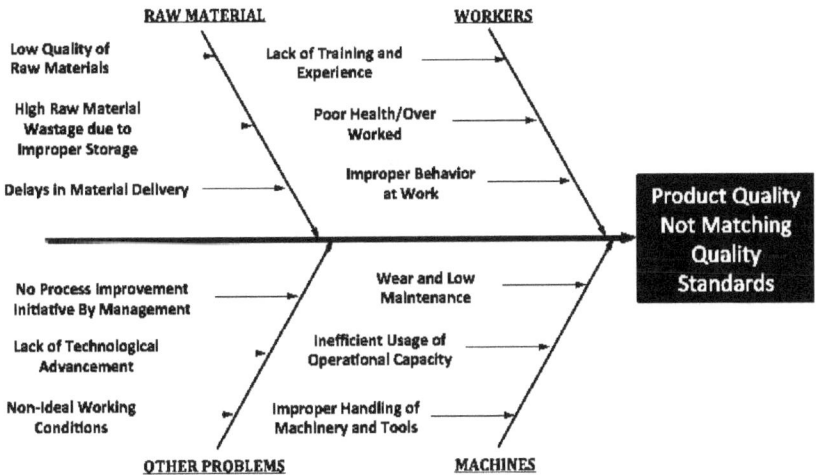

The Management Toolbox

The Cause & Effect Diagram was developed to represent the relationship between an "effect" and the possible causes. The effect or problem is stated on the right side of the chart as the fish's "head" and the major causes or influences are listed to the left at the end of each major "bone". Other causes that may create the major causes are then drawn off the major "bones". The causes are pushed back as far as possible, moving past symptoms, to find root causes.

Cause & Effect Diagrams are drawn to clearly illustrate the various causes affecting a process by sorting out and relating the causes. For every effect there are likely to be several major categories of causes. The major causes are often summarised under four categories – People, Method, Materials, Machinery – symbolizing those causes created by people such as inattentiveness or insufficient training; by methodology and procedures such as poor policies or procedures; materials such as incorrect components or poor quality materials; and machines and equipment such as slow equipment or poor technology.

These four standard categories of causes are only suggestions and other major categories may emerge in the analysis.

From this well-defined list of causes (and the causes of causes), the most likely are identified and chosen for further analysis using some of the other tools in this Toolbox.

Tips on constructing a Cause & Effect Diagram:

- Brainstorm possible major causes and agree on the categories such as People, Method, Materials and Machinery, then brainstorm the possible causes within those and other major categories;

- Construct the diagram.

- Use the "Five Why's" tool (page 66) to push back from the major causes as far as possible starting with the first question "why does this happen?"

- In interpretation, look for causes that appear repeatedly and if necessary gather data about the relative frequency of the different causes.

The Management Toolbox

Five Why's

When you need to drive understanding beyond the immediate response to get to the root of the matter.

The 5 Why's technique is a technique of iterative questioning about a particular condition so as to arrive at the root cause for the condition. It is most used to construct a Cause & Effect Diagram but has other uses in "getting to the bottom" of an issue.

The technique drills down by repeatedly asking "Why?"

The answer to each question forms the basis of the next question. The number 5 is settled upon as the appropriate number of times to ask the questions because of an empirical observation that the number of iterations required to get to the root cause of a problem is 5.

An example of the technique is as follows.

The problem is defined, for example "The laptop cannot access the internet."

1. Why is the laptop unable to access the internet? *Because the Wi-Fi signal has failed.*

2. Why has the Wi-Fi signal failed? *Because the Wi-Fi router is damaged.*

3. Why is the Wi-Fi router damaged? *Because it always blows up.*

4. Why does the router "always" blow up? *Because it is frequently subjected to electricity surges.*

5. Why is the router frequently subject to electricity surges? *Because the safety systems about plugging it into a surge protector are not followed.*

In this example it would have been easy to replace the router after the second question, but applying 5 Why's leads us to the root cause for a long term solution, thus eliminating the probability that the replaced router will continue to fail without the protection of a surge protector.

Tips on using 5 Why's:

- Avoid assumptions and instead trace the causality in direct increments through the symptoms to a root cause;

- Not all problems have a single root cause and you may have to repeat the process several times using a different sequence of questions – sometimes you may have to branch out after a couple of questions into several different sequences;

- Involve others who may have a deeper understanding of the problem – the person answering cannot go beyond their knowledge.

Scatter Diagram

When you need to display what happens to one variable when another variable changes.

A Scatter Diagram is used to study the possible relationship between one variable and another. It is used to test for possible cause and effect relationships. It cannot prove that a change in one variable *causes* a change in another but it does make it clear whether a relationship exists and the strength of that relationship.

A Scatter Diagram is constructed where the X-axis (horizontal) represents the measured values of one variable, and the Y-axis (vertical) represents the measurements of the other variable.

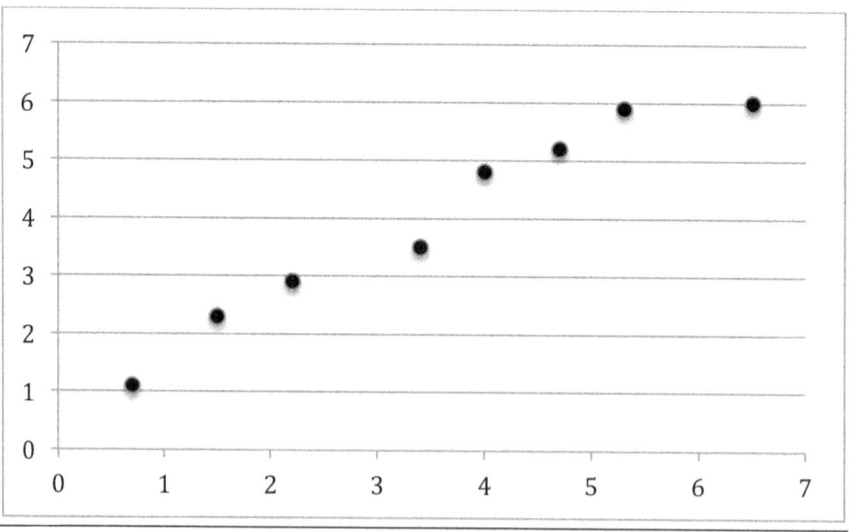

In the above example the plotted points form a pattern. The direction and "tightness" of the pattern provides an indication of the strength of the relationship between the horizontal X-axis variable (say Hours in this case) and the vertical Y-axis variable (say units produced).

In this example then we can see that as hours increase, more units are produced.

The more that this relationship resembles a straight line, the stronger is the relationship between the two variables.

Tips on construction and interpretation:

- A tight scatter close to a straight line indicates a close relationship;

- A looser scatter more or less in a line indicates a *possible* relationship;

- A loose scatter all over the page indicates no relationship;

- A negative relationship (the line slopes down from left to right) where as Y increases, X decreases, is as important as a positive relationship;

Venn Diagram

When you want to organise information visually so that you can see the relationships between several sets of items and what might be common amongst those sets.

A Venn Diagram depicts how different sets of items intersect and what is common amongst them against what is not common.

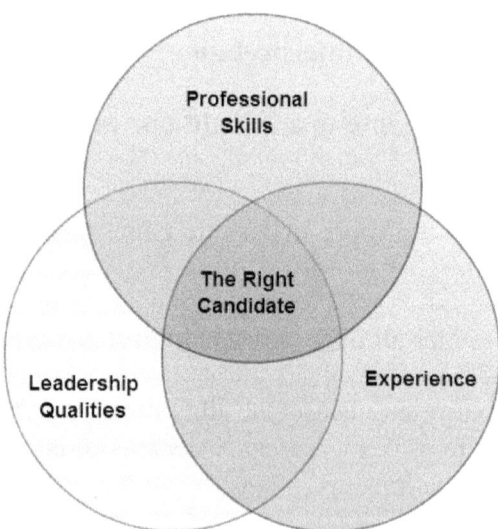

In this example used to compare the attributes of candidates for a job, the three attributes are Professional skills, Experience and

Leadership qualities represented by the circles. The intersection of all three circles is where the ideal candidate would lie. Any candidates in the intersection between Professional Skills and Experience would still lack the third required quality of Leadership. In the same way any candidate in the intersection between Experience and Leadership Qualities lacks Professional Skills, and any candidate in the intersection between Leadership Qualities and Professional Skills lacks Experience.

Tips on using Venn Diagrams:

- Identify the sets you want to analyse and brainstorm attributes of those sets;

- Identify any common attributes;

- Draw the circles and place the attributes in the appropriate areas of those circles – where they do not intersect (attribute that is not shared), and where they intersect;

- In interpreting them you can use them to compare and contrast or you can use them to classify – solutions can then be found in or for each area of the diagram.

Product Features and Benefits Analysis

When you need to market the difference between your product and that of your competition.

Features and Benefits are two sides of a product or service. In most cases when people are asked to describe their product, they tend to describe its features. However in marketing, customers tend to buy a product for the benefits it brings to them rather than its features.

Features of a product are the tangible or technical aspects of the product that make up what it is, or describes how it was made. Examples of features are:-

- "hand-crafted"
- "steel chassis"
- "latest CPU chip"
- "light weight material"

Benefits on the other hand are the attributes, largely emotive, that the customer thinks will benefit them as they arise from the features, and examples are:-

- "one-off example to display"
- "saves money on maintenance"

- "fast and saves time"
- "easy to carry"

Tips on Features and Benefits Analysis:

- Identify the product or service;
- List all the features of the product or service;
- For each feature, consider what benefits that might give the customer (put yourself in the shoes of the customer);
- Market the benefits.

The Management Toolbox

Customer Value Matrix

When you need to analyse the value of the customer to the business in order to prioritise service and resources.

A Customer Value Matrix depicts the value of the customer to you.

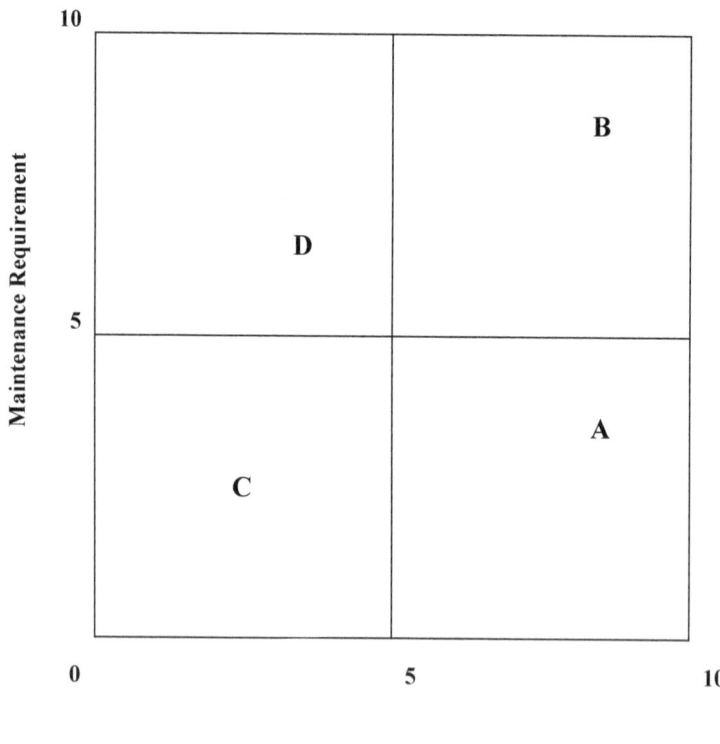

In the above example the matrix shows the profitability of a customer against the level of maintenance required to maintain the relationship.

Customer A in the bottom right quarter is a customer who does not need much effort to retain the relationship, and yet provides a high profit to the business. Customer A is a valuable customer and cost-effective nurturing should be provided to that customer.

Customer B in the top right quarter is a high profitability customer but needs a lot of relationship maintenance. Customer B is still valuable due to the profit that can be sustained, and resources to maintain the relationship need to be organised.

Customer C in the bottom left corner provides low profit to the business but also does not require much effort to maintain the relationship. Resources need not be allocated to Customer C, unless they can be moved to the bottom right quarter.

Customer D in the top left quarter is a low profitability customer yet requires high maintenance. Customer D can be avoided and allowed to leave.

Tips on using the Customer Value Matrix:

- Use common sense – it may be possible to change one variable to move the customer to another quadrant.

Developing Solutions

This next collection of tools are primarily useful when you are implementing solutions, whether you are making decisions about what solutions to implement, developing models for those solutions, or planning.

However what should be starting to emerge to you is that many of these management tools can be used in various stages of problem-solving, and several tools from the previous section can be used in this phase, as several tools here can be used in analysis.

Specifically, the following tools described under Analysing Issues can also be used for developing solutions:-

- Pie Chart (page 49)

- Brainstorming (page 21)

The Pareto Principle

When you need to identify which initiatives might have the greatest impact.

The Pareto Principle is also called the 80/20 Rule and refers to the observation that most things in life are not distributed evenly so that for example:-

- 80% of a firm's profits come from 20% of the customers;

- 80% of the outputs are produced by 20% of the workers;

- 80% of the defects are caused by 20% of the processes; and so on.

The Pareto Principle implies then that you should prioritise work on the 20% that creates the 80% of impact.

Tips on using the Pareto Principle:

- It is a principle not a rule! Statistically 80 plus 20 does not always add up to 100, sometimes 75% of the results are generated by 17% of the variables and the rest are "outliers" so use the principle as a guide, not a rule.

The Management Toolbox

Decision Tree

When you need to choose between a number of options.

A decision tree is a visual tool that helps you in making decisions between a number of viable options. It allows you to quantify the potential results of each option and includes the element of probability by allowing each option to have three possible results – Optimistic, Best Guess, and Pessimistic.

A decision tree is set out as follows:-

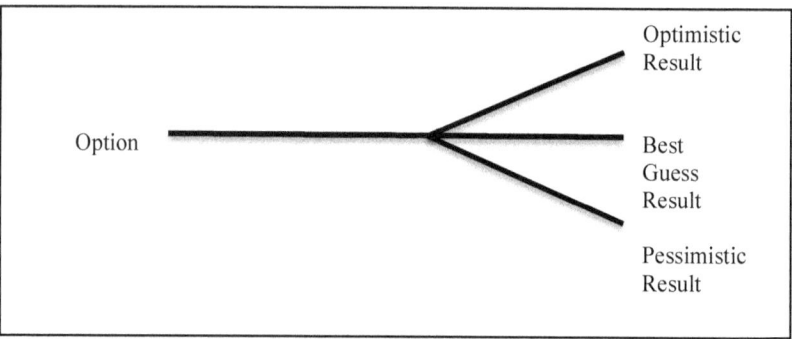

To show how this works, take an example of a legal firm that has to decide whether or not to merge with either of two other firms, or to do nothing.

To begin to work this out, they make some estimates:-

Option	Possible Result	Probability	Expected extra profit	Value (Probability X Expected extra profit)
Merge with Firm 1	Optimistic	30%	$250,000	$75,000
	Best Guess	50%	$100,000	$50,000
	Pessimistic	20%	$50,000	$10,000
	Total			**$135,000**
Merge with Firm 2	Optimistic	20%	$300,000	$60,000
	Best Guess	60%	$200,000	$120,000
	Pessimistic	20%	$100,000	$20,000
	Total			**$200,000**
Do nothing	Optimistic	15%	$50,000	$7,500
	Best Guess	80%	$0	$0
	Pessimistic	5%	-$100,000	-$5,000
	Total			**$2,500**

Shown in decisions trees, the results will show:-

The Management Toolbox

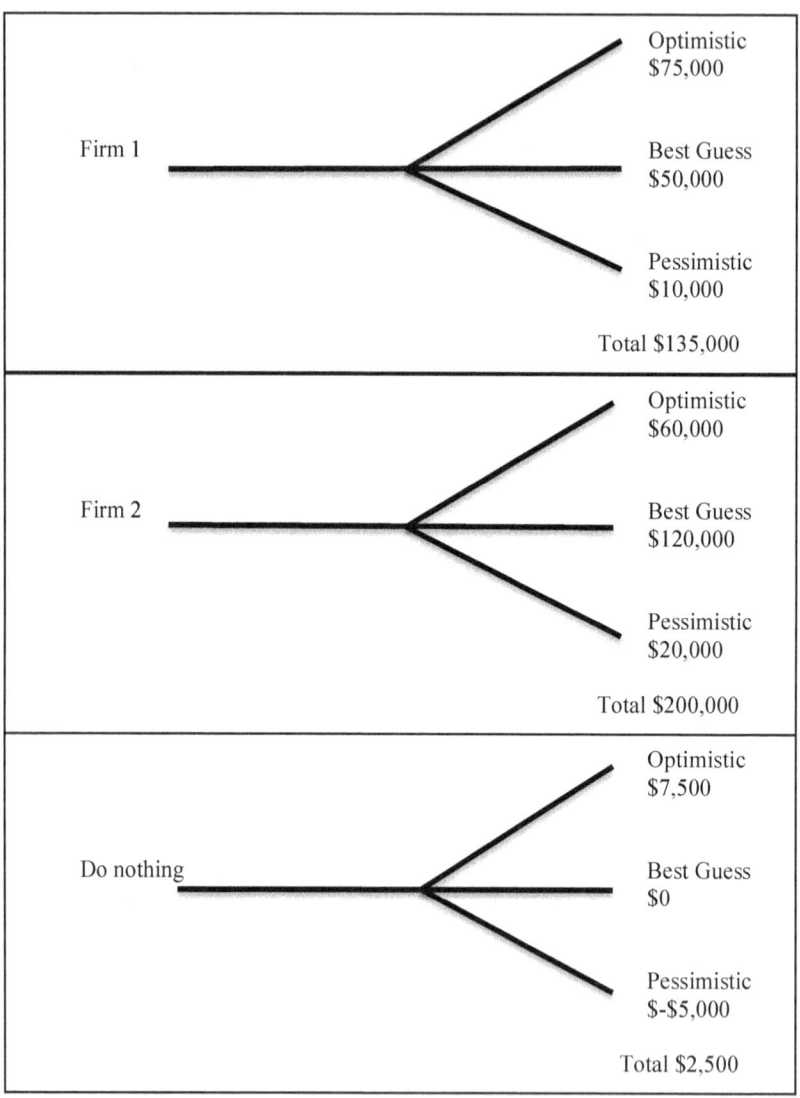

From the decision trees, it looks as if Firm 2 is the best option. This is despite the most optimistic possibility of Firm 1 seems better than the optimistic possibility of Firm 2. The inclusion of probabilities across optimistic, best guess and pessimistic provides a more complete picture.

Tips on using decision trees:-

- Decision trees are only one decision-making tool you should use – while the example above provides one answer to the decision, this has to be weighed against other factors such as the corporate cultures of the two firms, and in this case, whether any conflicts of interest arise as they put their two client lists together.

- Critical to the effectiveness of the decision tree is the estimates of the results in Optimistic, Best Guess, and Pessimistic positions, and in the estimate of the probability of their happening. These quantities are only estimates, but you need to ensure that as you estimate those of one option against another, you keep a level playing field and use the same assumptions.

007
The Product Development Process

When you need to manage the development of new products or services

Product development is an important part of any business, and can be a costly investment. The Product Development Process is a 6 step process that allows each step to "test" the idea and viability of the new product, thus forming a series of hurdles.

The Product Development Process starts, not with an objective to produce the new product, but rather with a flexible goal to test the product using each step as a hurdle.

The 6 steps in the Product Development Process are:-

1. Generate the idea
2. Test the concept
3. Prototype and product design
4. Product testing
5. Market testing
6. Product launch

The details of each step are discussed below.

Step 1 – Generate the idea

Refreshing your products or services is a critical activity in any business. So many businesses have gone out of business because they rested on their laurels after launching what they thought was a product that would never date.

Ideas for new products or innovations to your product come from a number of sources. The best source is the market which is always evolving and demanding new products; alternative sources include your industry, technology and the competition.

To get new ideas, listen to your customers about what they want and what they don't like about your product; listen to your salespeople about what they have heard about what their customers want; watch your competitors to see what they are doing; stay informed by your industry associations and keep abreast of changes to technology, legislation and other cultural factors.

If a new idea for a product does not meet the market, it is unlikely to be sensible to proceed further.

Step 2 – Test the concept

This is a form of market research. Having generated an idea and worked on it to describe it further, you can ask respondents (customers, associates, partners, or a market research company to run tests) a series of questions such as:-

- Do you have a need for this?

- What do you use now instead of this product?

The Management Toolbox

- How frequently would you use this product?
- What problems would this product solve for you?
- What would you change about this product?
- What would this product compete against?
- Would you buy?

You would only continue if market testing showed there was some demand for the new product.

Step 3 – Prototype and product design

In this step, your technical people are most involved in designing the product and constructing a prototype. In the case of a service, it would be the people usually involved in developing services or implementing them – for example a new accounting service would be designed by accountants.

However it is important that others are also involved to obtain varied views on practicality and viability. Marketing and Sales need to be involved to provide input on how the design might be seen by the market, and marketed. In manufacturing, the people in production should be involved to provide their input into how it can be manufactured at the right cost.

The hurdle in step 3 is to ensure the product design is cost-effective to produce and that the design is acceptable by the market.

A $100,000 toilet seat may be appropriate for the space shuttle, but not for the general market.

Step 4 – Product testing

Product testing aims to answer issues like:-

- Does it actually work?

- Can customers use it appropriately?

- Will it fall apart if used under expected conditions?

These are product related issues and marketing issues are dealt with later.

Product tests are conducted just before production to ensure that the product works as it is supposed to work. In technology users are often invited to partake in a Beta Test of new software, whereas in some other areas, product tests involve recruiting volunteers to use the products or the products are field tested in their own offices.

Step 5 – Market testing

Once the product is shown to be capable of being used as it is designed to be used, it can be market tested.

Sometimes companies run both product testing and market testing at the same time, however care should be taken if you do this because they have different intended outcomes and you should not confuse the two.

The Management Toolbox

The outcome of market testing is not about the usability of the product but the acceptability of it in the market. Market testing gives you information about pricing points and placement in the market.

Market testing involves getting responses to questions like:-

- Would you buy it?
- What price is acceptable?
- Responses to packaging, advertisements, product literature
- Where would you buy it from?

Step 6 – Product launch

Product launches can take several different routes.

For example in the hospitality industry there are often soft launches before the hard launch. A soft launch is the launch of the product without significant marketing, and often it helps "iron out the kinks". A hard launch usually includes the main marketing thrust including guest appearances and so on.

Product launches can be gradual, say starting only in certain stores or cities, or across selected customers. Or launches can be immediate with a blaze of publicity.

Tips on the Product development Process:-

- The 6 steps should be viewed as hurdles, not a plan – be mentally prepared to pull the product if it does not get over the hurdle of any step.

- Be aware of the need to involve cross-functional teams in product development – there have been many technically great products that have not sold well, something the marketing people could have foreseen.

- Be aware of the need for external expertise, especially during market testing – budget accordingly.

The Management Toolbox

Customer Attractiveness Matrix

When you need to prioritise customers by their attractiveness to your business in order to prioritise marketing efforts.

The Customer Attractiveness Matrix is a way of categorizing your customers or markets into four major categories.

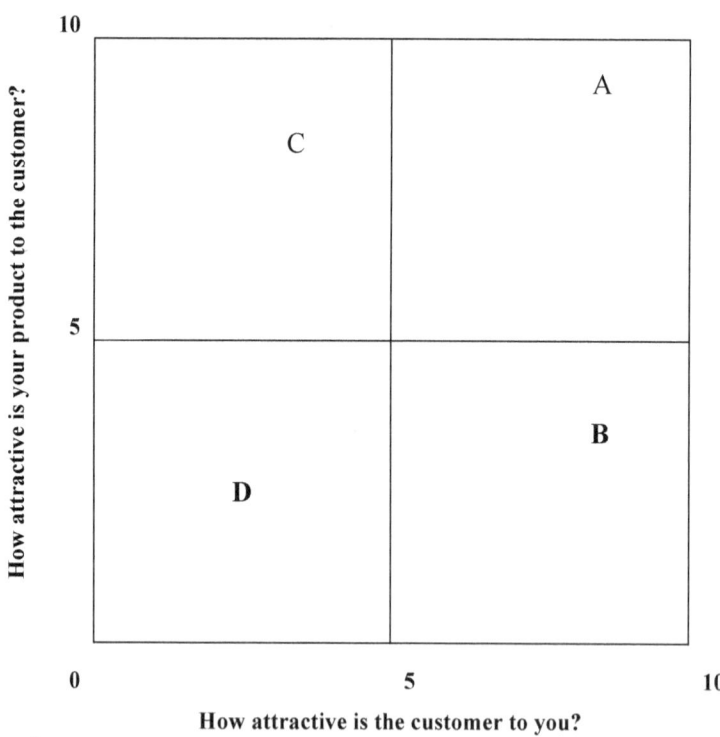

The Customer Attractiveness Matrix compares two factors:-

- How attractive is the customer (or market segment) to you – by valuing profitability, ease of access, and so on; and

- How attractive is the product to your customer (or market segment) – measured by their need for the product benefits, your brand attractiveness, and so on.

These factors are scored from 0 to 10 (where 10 is the most attractive) against each customer and plotted on the matrix.

In the example above Customer A is a target customer because he or she is attractive to the business and will find the product attractive themselves. Not only is that customer valuable to the business but since the product will be attractive to them it will be easier to market to them.

Customer B is attractive to the business but may not be as attracted to the product. Although it will be harder to market to this person, you can analyse why the product is not as attractive to them and plan to change that view, resulting in the customer moving to the top right quadrant.

Customer C finds the product attractive, but for whatever reason (perhaps profitability) is less attractive to the business. The strategy for this type of customer is to "maintain" without expending a lot of resources, while attempting to eliminate the reason they are not as attractive to you, hence moving them into the top right quadrant as well.

The Management Toolbox

Customer D does not find the product attractive nor is attractive to the business – ignore this category of customer.

Tips on using the Customer Attractiveness Matrix:

- List all your customers or market segments and then allocate scores for attractiveness to you and their attraction to the product out of 10, not allowing a score of 5 (if necessary decide between 4.5 and 5.5)

- Be aware of exceptions – a customer may be scored into a lower priority quadrant, but there may be some reason such as potential, that may require you to suspend the usual rules

Teik P Oh

Affinity Diagram

When you need to organise large amounts of information and ideas into groups based on logical relationships.

Affinity Diagrams were originally drawn, but since the advent of the Post-it Note, are usually constructed using these notes.

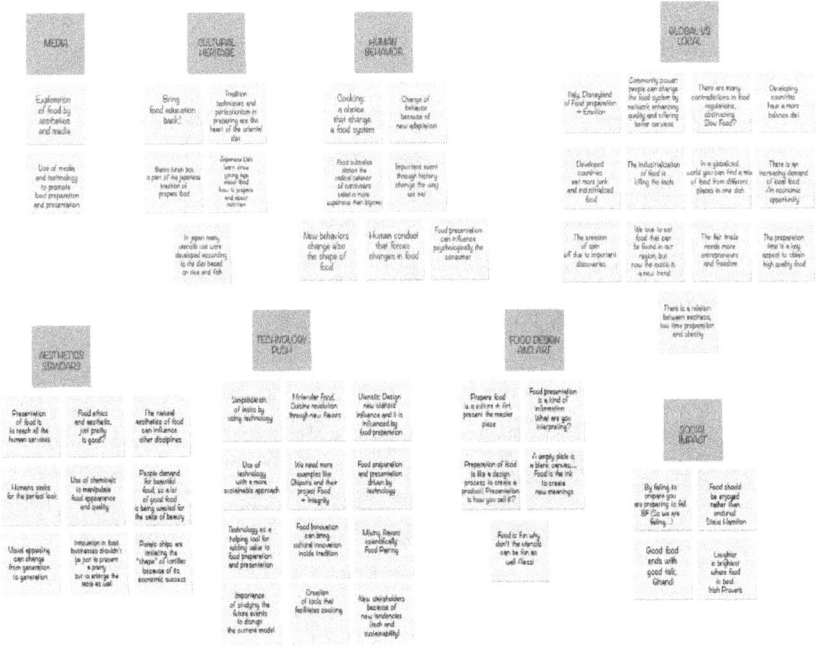

An Affinity Diagram is really useful when you are confronted with a potentially overwhelming set of ideas, information and planning steps, and particularly useful as a Brainstorming tool.

It can also be used in the analysis of a problem by collecting results from interviews and data gathering.

The Affinity Diagram is used in the following way:-

1. All the ideas are individually recorded on Post-it Notes or index cards;

2. An initial review identifies common themes or groups;

3. These identified groupings are named and header Post-it Notes or index cards are labeled;

4. The individual ideas are grouped under the headers accordingly;

5. Larger clusters may be organised into sub-groups;

6. Each sub-group and group is then reviewed so that the individual Post-it Notes or index cards are arranged in some order within the groups;

7. A permanent diagram is then drawn and recorded.

Tips on using Affinity Diagrams:

- The best results are often achieved when brainstormed in a cross-functional team.

- Make notes of comments and ideas that are "off-topic" that emerge during discussions – constructing an Affinity Diagram often immerses the participants deeply in the process which can reveal useful insights not directly related to the issue.

Crossover Analysis

When you need to identify a point when it might be better to switch from one piece of equipment to another one that appears to have the same benefits but have different fixed and variable costs.

You can also use Crossover Analysis to decide between two comparable products or services you sell but which have different fixed and variable costs.

The formula is:-

Crossover Units = (Option 2 Fixed Costs – Option 1 Fixed Costs)/(Option 1 Variable Costs – Option 2 variable Costs).

Take an example where a factory has to choose between two machines producing widgets.

Machine 1 has fixed costs of $100,000 and variable costs of $2 per widget made.

Machine 2 has fixed costs of $50,000 and variable costs of $4 per widget made.

Which machine you buy will depend on the number of widgets you will produce, so the first step of Crossover Analysis is to calculate the crossover point, or the point at which the number of widgets made by both machines will have an equivalent cost.

Using the above formula, crossover point is:-

(50,000-100,000)/(2-4) = (-50,000)/(-2) = 25,000 widgets

When you make 25,000 widgets the cost of producing those widgets is the same if you use Machine 1 or Machine 2.

Above and below 25,000 widgets produced, one machine is preferable to the other.

To find out which one is better, calculate the cost of producing widgets just below and just over 25,000 units.

If you produce 24,000 units,

Machine 1 costs (24,000x$2)+$100,000 = $148,000

Machine 2 costs (24,000x$4)+$50,000 = $146,000

So, when you produce less than 25,000 widgets, Machine 2 will cost you less.

However if you produced 26,000 units then,

Machine 1 costs (26,000x$2)+$100,000 = $152,000

Machine 2 costs (26,000x$4)+$50,000 = $154,000

So if you produce more than 25,000 widgets, Machine 1 is cheaper to use.

Using Crossover Analysis you now know that if you produce less than 25,000 widgets you should buy Machine 2 and if you produce more than 25,000 widgets you should buy Machine 1. You can then make your purchasing decision based on your forecast of the demand for widgets.

Tips for using Crossover Analysis:

- Remember that this analysis ignores any differences between the quality of products produced by the two machines;

- You may need to use Crossover Analysis in conjunction with Break-even Analysis – in the example, although it is cheaper to produce 24,000 widgets with Machine 2, you still have to sell each widget for more than $6.08 ($146,000/24,000) per unit, and you will need to work out what your selling price needs to be to recover all your costs including overheads;

- You will need to be able to forecast the volume of sales with some accuracy.

Training Matrix

When you need to develop staff training and identify the best training method for the occasion.

A training matrix recognises and illustrates the four main training types:-

- Formal Training
- Informal Training
- On the Job Training
- Off the Job Training.

When you are planning training for your team, you can use the training matrix to identify the best type of training that is appropriate for the team member and skill-type.

The Management Toolbox

	On the Job	Off the Job
Formal	Classroom Assignments Projects	Workshops Online video etc. Study groups
Informal	Mentor programs Coaching Self-study	Social groups Networking Reading

Tips on using the Training Matrix:

- Use a combination of all types.

Management Presentation

When you need to present your findings or plans.

At some stage in management, after analysis, problem-solving, planning and implementation, you will need to present the ideas and plans to some stakeholder group, whether that be owners, senior management, or the rest of the team. These presentations start the change journey and need to provide information and solutions in a way that convinces and "sells" to people.

A checklist for such a presentation is:-

- Decide who are the appropriate stakeholders (or groups of stakeholders) to make one or more presentations to;

- Invite the stakeholders to the presentation(s) by an appropriate method (memo, personal invitation, announcement) and follow up the day before;

- Arrange for the venue (right size, right atmosphere);

- Arrange for any equipment (audio-visual, flip charts, whiteboards);

- Decide which charts would help to present the information;

- Prepare the charts (PowerPoint or Keynote), keeping them limited in number but succinct;

- If appropriate assign presentation roles and responsibilities;

- Before the presentation check the room and test the equipment.

Tips for Management Presentation:

- Ensure you know the objective of the presentation (to inform, to obtain a decision, to obtain buy-in) and work to that objective and no other

- Speak clearly and slowly (rehearse!)

- Summarise any decisions or recommendations and provide written follow up

Business Model Canvas

The Business Model Canvas was developed by Alexander Osterwalder as a visualization model that places all the aspects of your business on one page or "canvas".

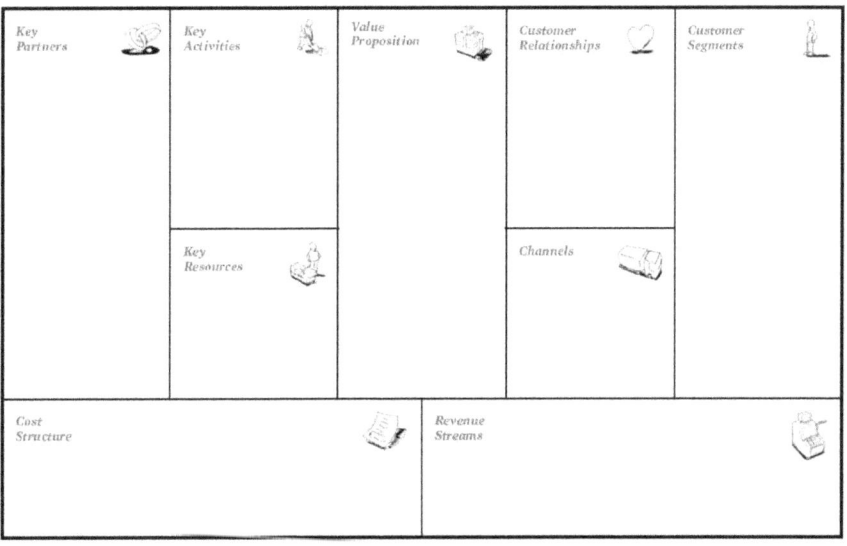

The canvas incorporates sections dealing with:-

- Value propositions
- Customer relationships
- Customer segments
- Channels

The Management Toolbox

- Key activities
- Key partners
- Key resources
- Cost structure
- Revenue streams

Using these building blocks, you develop a concept for your business model in a way that ensures each aspect of your business is in sync with the other aspects. The Business Model Canvas has been variously described as a visual Business Plan, a Brand concept, and a simple explanation of your business' world.

More details can be found at www.businessmodelgeneration.com or from Osterwalder and Yves Pigneur's book *Business Model Generation*.

Tips on using the Business Model Canvas:

- Read the book!

Quality Circles

When you need to increase the quality of your processes.

Quality circles involve representatives from across different teams in your organisation. As a quality circle, they meet regularly to discuss any problems over quality, the reasons for those problems, and any potential solutions. The cross-functionality of the quality circle means that problems arising from many sources can be heard. For example unless Salespeople are involved, the people from production might not realise that the packaging breaks up when it is delivered.

Quality circles push responsibility for fixing problems down to the people who can be directly affected, whether in production, service or sales, and those people are the most likely to be able to provide practical solutions.

Quality circles create more involvement by all members of the team, higher morale and pride in their work.

Tips on quality circles:-

- Quality circles primarily discuss issues around production of the product or service but it is important to include representatives from other departments such as sales and purchasing for their input.

The Management Toolbox

- They need to meet regularly with a set agenda for discussion, incorporating reporting back on previous solutions suggested.

Organisation Charts

When you need to organise relationships between teams and team members and reporting hierarchies.

An organisation chart is a diagram that shows the relationship between one worker with another, or one team or department with another. It also represents who has authority over whom.

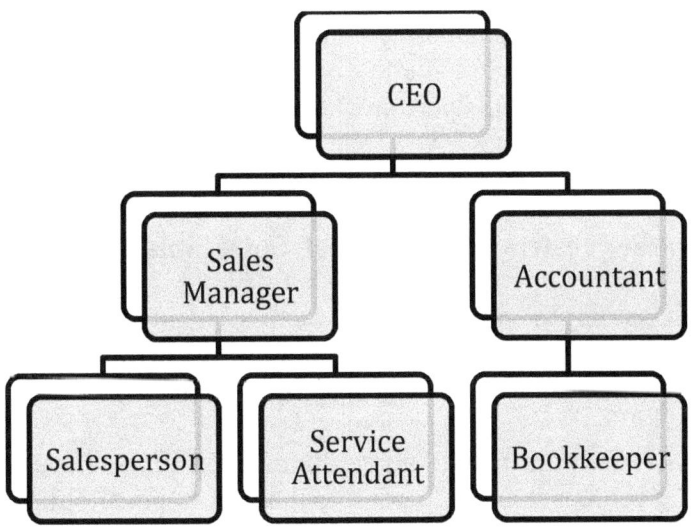

The Management Toolbox

An organisation chart clarifies roles and responsibilities, especially when used with Job Descriptions. Constructing an organisation chart allows you to identify and create logical relationships that may not seem obvious until drawn up, and allows you to reorganize functions to better suit day to day efficiency.

In Michael Gerber's book *The E-Myth* he postulates that you should draw up your completed organisation chart incorporating all the roles and responsibilities in your business as separate positions, even if you are starting up with only one or two employees. This allows you to identify individually important roles that might otherwise be forgotten and incorporated into one person. This also allows you to grow seamlessly and add people into existing "positions" and all you then have to do is hand over the corresponding responsibilities from the person who originally did everything.

Tips on the construction and use of an Organisation Chart:

- Use only position titles, do not use names of individuals – this allows you to separate the characteristics and skills of an individual from what a position might need

- Ensure you include all positions even if you have to mark several as "vacant" and note that the responsibilities of that person are currently being allocated to another

Job Descriptions

When you need to specify the roles and responsibilities (and performance expectations) of team members.

A job description is a personalised list of roles, responsibilities and duties of a worker. It will often include who the person reports to/who reports to the person, requirements such as skills and experience, and performance measures. Job descriptions clarify and avoid disputes, aid performance review, and add to Organisation Charts by explaining how the relationships operate.

A standard job description template may consist of:-

- Position Title

- Employee's Name

- Position Overview – describing general role within the organisation and objectives of the position

- Working Relationships – nominating the person this position reports to and a list of positions that report to this role

- Principal Responsibilities – listing the main responsibilities of this position (e.g. "Providing accurate financial reports" or "Sales management", and detailing them as necessary with a list of duties under each responsibility (e.g. "Entering transactions daily, preparing bank reconciliations, checking balances for accuracy" or "Scheduling sales visits by salespeople, follow up on sales enquiries"

- Key Performance Measures – listing of measures by which the position will be evaluated against

- Position Requisites – list any required skills, qualifications and experience

Tips on Job Descriptions:

- Write the job description for the role – never write a job description to fit an individual's skills. Writing a job description to fit an incumbent creates the risk of leaving out key responsibilities, or adding them to an inappropriate position. If necessary, one person may have two or more job descriptions for multiple roles as long as the duties do not conflict. This recognises that in some circumstances, one person may have responsibilities that are across more than one position, and allows those responsibilities to be handed on when the second position is filled.

- The list of Key Performance Measures should be short and objectively measurable by means that do not require disproportionate reporting mechanisms. They should be measures that are "key" to the achievement of the outcomes required by that position, not a list of measures of each duty and responsibility.

Policies and Procedures

When you need to create efficiency by defining the principles the business will operate under, and how certain operations are conducted.

Policies and procedures create efficiency because once recorded, they form the "rules" by which the business will operate so that you don't have to reinvent the wheel each time a key operation is undertaken. New staff can fit into the processes by reading the policies and procedures and understanding what the limits of what they do are and how to do it.

Policies are statements of how the organisation will conduct its business and provide guidance for day-to-day decisions. For example a policy may be to "maintain the highest work health and safety standards".

Procedures describe how various operations under the policies will be carried out. For example under the above health and safety policy, there may be procedures for fire and emergencies, accident-reporting, etc. Each procedure should outline:-

- Who will do what;
- The steps to be taken;
- Any forms or documents to use.

The Management Toolbox

The process to develop policies and procedures is:-

1. Identify the need for a policy (either anticipating a need because of new activities or changing circumstances, or responding to a need that becomes apparent from some confusion);

2. Gather information and draft the policy (use the SMART tool to assess);

3. Consider what procedures are required. What clear guidance or even step by step instructions will be required to carry out the policy. For example a complaints policy will need procedures on receiving, recording, reporting and following up on complaints.

4. Consult with stakeholders and users of the intended policy and procedures;

5. Finalise/approve the policy and procedures;

6. Implement;

7. Monitor, review and revise.

Tips on Policies and Procedures:

- It is always easy to accidentally create a policy, or more likely a procedure, that conflicts with another – take your time to review for conflicts.

- Collate policies and procedures in a manual, and if possible put this online and make them searchable for key words.

- There are various software packages and online resources to help you write policies and procedures – MAUS (www.maus.com.au) have been marketing theirs for a long time now and have a great deal of experience in the area of automating manuals.

Force Field Analysis

When you need to identify the forces that might either drive or restrain change in a new initiative.

Force Field Analysis was developed by Kurt Lewin, who proposed that change occurs only when there are sufficient dynamic forces influencing the situation. These forces could be either "driving forces" that move a situation toward change, or "restraining forces" that block movement. When there is insufficient driving force a status quo is maintained, no matter how bad the situation.

The use of Force Field Analysis is therefore to identify sets of driving and restraining forces on a given situation so that you can work to reinforce driving forces and reduce restraining forces. Force Field Analysis helps make change happen because:-

- It forces people to think together about all the facets of the desired change and encourage creative thinking;

- It encourages people to come to a consensus about the relative priority of factors on both sides of the change "balance sheet" (using tools such as Nominal Group Technique); and

- It provides a starting point for action.

To prepare a Force Field Analysis, draw the "balance sheet" for a given situation, and write the plan or proposal for change in the centre. Then list all the driving forces on the left, and the restraining forces on the right.

Score each force, say 1 (weak) to 5 (strong) and add up the total scores of the driving forces, and of the restraining forces. This will give you an indication of the imbalance, as well as which forces are the significant ones. An example of a Force Field Analysis chart is as follows:-

Figure 1:
Force Field Analysis

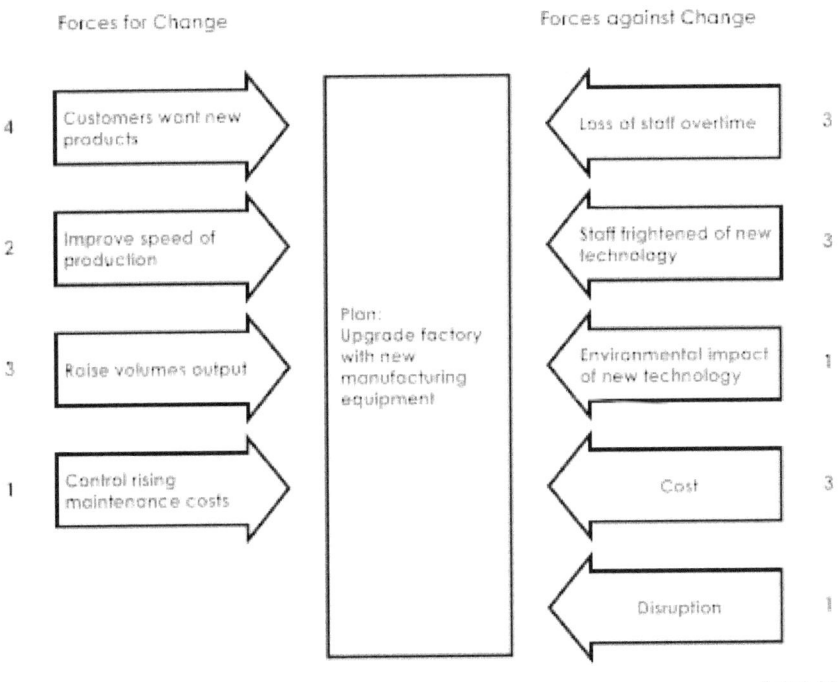

The Management Toolbox

The Force Field Analysis can help you decide whether or not to go ahead with the change by showing you the pressure for and against change; or to plan for successful change by strengthening the forces driving change while weakening those restraining change.

Tips for using Force Field Analysis:

- Strengthening the positive sometimes has the unexpected result of reinforcing the negative. Take for example someone being told that exercise is good for them – instead of improved performance this can sometimes increase resistance. Some studies show that a more effective tactic is to diminish or eliminate a restraining force.

- Identify as many forces as possible, involve as many people as possible in developing the list as the forces affecting them may be different from those affecting you.

Vision and Mission Statements

When you need to describe the central idea of the organisation, answering questions such as what it does and why it does that.

These types of statements are sometimes called Mission, Vision and Values Statements, or Purpose, Vision and Values Statements, or some variation. They generally include a short description of the vision of the organisation, its purpose or mission, and the set of values by which it exists.

These statements provide a tool to define and guide your organisation's journey to its desired future.

A Vision Statement is a description of the future your organisation wants to create. It describes the long term state if it is successful. Some examples of Vision Statements are:-

- *Our vision is to provide every business with the tools they need to grow*

- *We will be the world's leading provider of ethical investments*

- *Our company is working to lead the way in developing sustainable communities alongside our mining activities*

A Mission (or Purpose) Statement describes what it does to achieve the vision. An organisation's Mission Statement is all about what it does. Some examples are:-

- *We develop the most advanced business software for all types of businesses*

- *We research and study investment platforms against financial and ethical measurements to find the best ethical investments throughout the world, in order to benefit individual and institutional investors*

- *We seek, develop, and operate mining operations in Australia; we employ and train people to become contributors; we strive to be good corporate partners with local communities*

A Values Statement is a list of guiding principles which underpin the organisation. They represent what really matters to your organisation and which guide how things are done. Some examples are:-

- *Do no harm*

- *Quality, Collaboration, Inquiry*

- *Service beyond expectations*

Your Vision, Mission and Values Statement should drive everything in the organisation – planning should be measured against it, day to day activity should be guided by it.

In his book *Leading Change*, John Kotter notes that a well-crafted Vision Statement removes the need to manage every small day-to-day decision. If it is clear and understood, people simply ask themselves if what they are about to do corresponds with the Vision and helps the organisation achieve the Vision, and make their own decision.

Tips on Vision, Mission, Values Statements:

- Adopting the Vision, Mission, Values Statement starts from the top – management leaders need to show that they are following the guidance of the statement on a daily basis, and as necessary, refer to it in the decisions they make.

- Reward people for the way they use the Vision, Mission, Values Statement as guidance for their work.

- Vision statements need to look sufficiently far into the future so as to create enough of a challenge to get there.

- Qualify the values. People often make the mistake of including socially agreed values as company values – for example "honesty and transparency." If you include it, does it mean that otherwise you would naturally behave dishonestly and opaquely? Test your values by seeing if it makes sense to include the opposite.

Strategic Planning

When you need to provide a high-level direction into the medium and longer term growth of the organisation.

Strategic planning is a useful management tool to outline a direction of the business over the longer term, towards achievement of its vision, and providing milestones for measuring the success of the journey.

Strategic planning is a high-level activity, providing goals and strategies but without substantial detail. Its purpose is to create a strategic direction over a less predictable longer term, and allow detailed business planning to take place over the more predictable shorter term. Typically strategic plans look at achieving long term horizons of 10 or more years, but actually plan for the first 5 or so years of that horizon. These are then used to guide the detailed annual business plans.

The strategic planning process involves defining "where do we want to be?", assessing "where are we now?", and then describing "how do we get there from here?"

The stages of strategic planning are:-

- Define the future by quantifying the vision – from the Vision, Mission, Values statement, quantify what the achievement of the vision actually means by looking at the end-state from different perspectives. Ask questions like "how will we look, behave, work, once we have achieved our Vision?"

- Conduct a situational analysis – describe the current situation. This is usually done through a process of workshops and consultations with key stakeholders including those outside the organisation. The tools used include SWOT (page 45) and PESTLE (page 43), market surveys, competitive and industry surveys, and review of the organisation's literature and constitutional documents.

- Analysing the gap – through a study of the current situation and the desired state, identify what restraints exist and what may have to be done. At the end of this analysis, key strategic issues are identified. These are key issues that the organisation has to resolve in order to bridge the gap.

- Agree Goals and Objectives – analysing key strategic issues, agree on the goals that should be achieved over the next 5 years to resolve the Key Strategic Issues and move satisfactorily along the strategic direction to the achievement of the vision. Goals are broad milestone achievements, objectives are the concrete attainments required to achieve the goal. For example a goal might be "To increase our market by 20% in 5 years" and objectives of that goal might be "Open three more stores per year; Introduce five more products into the marketplace per annum."

- From the Goals and Objectives, and keeping the vision in mind, formulate strategies to be carried out over the next 5 years. Strategies are the broad activities or initiatives required to meet the objectives. A strategy to meet the objective of opening more stores might be "to expand nationally."

Tips on Strategic Planning:

- Consult widely, focus planning.

- Keep considerations at a helicopter view – remember this is a strategic plan providing broad direction. Looking far ahead you will not have enough certainty to detail every strategy, however you can set direction.

- Build in reporting and measurement mechanisms – it is too easy to prepare a strategic plan and then leave it on a shelf.

- Avoid defining prescriptive Key Performance Indicators – these are more appropriately deal with at the Business Plans or operational planning level where the shorter timeframes allow more accurate forecasting and hence KPI setting.

- Strategic Planning is conducted at the owner, Board and senior management levels because it sets long term strategic direction. Involving middle management and other staff may detract from the need for strategic thinking over a longer timeframe and encourage operationally detailed considerations too early in the planning process. Staff input is sought after strategic direction is set to assist in how shorter-term goals and objectives can be prioritised to assist in achieving the long-term direction.

Business Planning

When you need to provide detailed plans on growing the business in the strategic direction.

A business plan is a documented set of goals, objectives, target market intentions, operational intentions, and financial forecasts. The difference between the goals and objectives of a business plan and those of a strategic plan is the term. The goals and objectives of a business plan are set to be achievable over a short term, such as one year.

A business plan is typically the detailed planning for the achievement of part of the way of a longer term strategic plan. Over the shorter period the variables are more predictable and hence a business plan can contain a lot of detail of the steps to be taken and the financial outcomes.

A business plan can satisfy a number of purposes and hence should be structured and written accordingly. The purposes include internal planning to follow the direction of a strategic plan, and to obtain finance or further investment.

The contents of a business plan may change depending on the purpose but is typically:-

- Executive Summary
- Vision, Mission, Values

The Management Toolbox

- Company Background (if external focus)
- Long (from strategic plan) and short term goals and objectives
- Product/Service – description, features, benefits, and development plans
- Marketing
    - Industry overview (particularly if external focus)
    - Target market
    - Competition
    - Marketing Plans
- Operations
    - Key personnel
    - Organisation chart
    - Human resources plan
    - Product/service delivery plan
    - Capital equipment plan
- Finances (summary)
- Monitoring and evaluation

- Appendices
  - Detailed financials
  - Other appendices

Tips on Business Plans:-

- Start with your long term outcomes. If you haven't written a strategic plan, at least work out what your Vision, Mission, Values statement is (page 115), and what it says the business will look like in the long term. Assess all plans against this long term direction to see if you are moving in the right direction.

- Decide on the time frame – 1 to 5 years. As this is a detailed plan it needs to be in a shorter time frame as the ability to be clear and certain about different situations becomes difficult beyond 2 or 3 years.

- Write the Executive Summary last – it is not an introduction, it is a short summary of everything else for the "lazy" reader or gatekeeper to make them interested in reading the rest.

… The Management Toolbox

Scenario Analysis

When you need to make decisions based on alternative possibilities.

Scenario Analysis improves decision-making by considering alternative scenarios and allowing the consideration of their probable outcomes and implications. Scenario Analysis does not predict the future but rather develops several possible scenarios based around a central starting point, and examining what might happen at certain turning points. Typically no more than 3 or 4 most likely scenarios are generated, taking into account, optimistic, pessimistic and most likely scenarios.

Scenario Analysis starts with a problem or a point in time and asks what might result from this position. For example the stated issue might be whether or not to expand a business into a new country. Answers to the question of what might result need to be based on known facts, for example political instability in that country. The answers generated might be 1) The expansion is relatively trouble free for the first year, 2) The expansion takes place and a military coup occurs in the first year, and 3) The expansion meets stiff competition. Each of those outcomes is then examined for a turning point and consideration takes place as to what might happen then, arriving at 1 to 3 possible outcomes resulting from the turning points.

In the above example the turning point for possibility 1) might be the end of the first year and due to known political circumstances at that turning point the possibilities might be 1) That the expansion continues without problems, 2) That the military coup takes place after the first year, and 3) That the competition is slow to take traction but starts to affect sales.

Once the Scenario Analysis arrives at the several possible endpoints, a review is conducted to choose the most likely or the most desirable to help make the decision. The Scenario Analysis can also be used to prepare plans to protect against the worst case scenarios.

A well-generated and described Scenario Analysis is incredibly powerful in equipping the business with rehearsed strategies and prepared decisions at different turning points, as well as in guiding strategy.

Tips on using Scenario Analysis:

- Take care to base scenario generation on facts rather than opinions.

- Depending on the complexity of the problem and the amount of known facts and high probability assumptions, Scenario Analysis can be extremely complicated and will need several iterations to generate scenarios – do not rush the process.

The Management Toolbox

Action Planning

When you need to prepare detailed plans for any action.

Action Plans exist under many names. All of them describe the act of making detailed step-by-step plans to implement any project, action or initiative.

This Action Planning process is based on a documented approach to describing what is being planned, what steps need to be taken, who leads each step, when the step has to be completed by, and what is the expected outcome from completing the step.

It is recorded using a worksheet such as the following:-

ACTION PLAN TO _____

Step No.	Detail	Leader	Date by	Expected Outcome
1				
2				
3				
4				

Tips on preparing Action Plans:

- Work backwards by first agreeing what the overall outcome of the action will need to look like.

- Brainstorm (page 21) all the steps that are required to implement the action, and then put them into logical time order.

- The "Leader" is not the person doing the tasks but the person who is responsible to see that it gets done, on time, and achieving the expected outcome. They co-ordinate and may delegate, but take ultimate responsibility in completing the tasks.

- When allocating the date each step is to be completed by, work backwards by first establishing if there is any deadline that has to be met. Before agreeing to the final dates, consider if there are any other commitments outside of this Action Plan.

- Use SMART (page 17) to review the Action Plan.

The Management Toolbox

Critical Path Analysis

When you need to plan the implementation of a project, where the various steps may need the completion of other steps before it can proceed any further, in the shortest time possible.

Critical Path Analysis creates a project model that shows the path from the start to the end of a project, taking into account the different tasks or activities that have to be completed, the dependencies between the activities where one may depend on one or more others to be completed first, the shortest and longest time each activity will take, and the "critical path" or the shortest possible time between start and end.

The analysis starts with gathering information about the project:-

1. The list of all the activities required to complete the project;

2. The longest time and the shortest time that each activity will take;

3. The dependencies between activities ("B must start after A ends, C must start after A ends but may start before B ends").

Using these values a Critical Path Analysis diagram is drawn showing the paths from start to finish:-

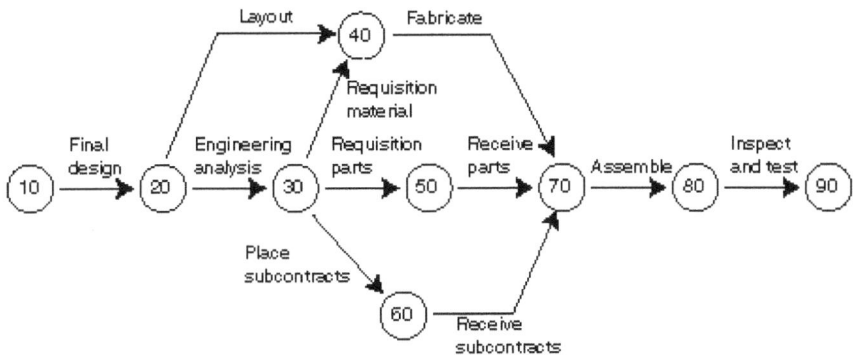

There are online and software based Critical Path Analysis project management tools that you can use to create your project plan and critical path. One example is Microsoft Project.

Tips for using Critical Path Analysis:

- The analysis shows the earliest time an activity can start as well as the latest time. The difference can create "slack" being the time that activity may have to wait until a predecessor task is completed. Be cautious in announcing the slack in the project as people may be tempted to use it without your knowledge.

- Some tasks that are non-critical may still require careful management.

Sales Component Analysis

When you need to make any sales increase target more achievable.

Sales targets often seem difficult to achieve from the quantum that is set. For a $1 million business a sales increase target of 20% means an increase of $200,000. This can appear unrealistic and unachievable, especially if the average sale amount is a few hundred dollars.

However analysing your sales by the three components breaks the target into three potentially more achievable targets.

All sales are made up of:-

- The average value of a sales transaction;
- The number of customers; and
- The average number of times a customer buys.

For example, the business with $1 million sales per annum might find that their sales is made up of:-

- An average value per sale of $100
- Selling to 5,000 customers in the year

- Who, on average, buy 2 times a year.

Their total sales is made up of

Average value per sale x No. of customers x Average No. of times they buy

or

$100 x 5,000 x 2 = $1,000,000

In order to increase sales by 20% you only have to increase *one* of these components by 20% so that either:-

1. $120 x 5,000 x 2 = $1,200,000 or

2. $100 x 6,000 x 2 = $1,200,000 or

3. $100 x 5,000 x 2.4 = $1,200,000

Using Sales Component Analysis your sales target can be met if you either

- increased the selling price from $100 to $120, or

- Increased the number of customers from 5,000 to 6,000, or

- Increased the number of times a customer bought from 2 times a year to 2.4 times a year.

The original, apparently unachievable sales target starts to look achievable because of the relatively small increases of each of the components. If the individual increases still appear unrealistic, you can increase each component by a smaller amount, and they leverage (multiply) to the target.

For example, the following smaller increases of each component achieves the same result:-

- Increase average value per sale by only $5 (5%) from $100 to $105, *and*

- Increase the number of customers by only 195 people (3.9%) from 5,000 to 5,195, *and*

- Increase the average number of times they buy by only 10% from twice a year to 2.2 times a year

$105 x 5,195 x 2.2 = $1,200,045

The smaller individual increases become achievable and you can plan how to increase each accordingly.

Tips on Sales Component Analysis:

- Use average values and if you can't find the exact values for the components of your sales, get to the nearest approximations. For example if you are unable to work out how many customers you have in a retail business, drop the period to a week and count the number of customers in that week. If you are unable to work out the average number of times a customer buys then assume each buys only once and count each sale as a new customer.

Five P's of Marketing

When you need to ensure that your marketing is using the different marketing elements in the correct mix.

"Marketing mix" refers to the combination of the five different marketing elements in a way that provides the best marketing strategy for the product.

The marketing mix is made up of the five P's which are:-

- Product – Quality? Needs fulfilled? Scarcity? Use? Features? Benefits?

- Price – High? Medium? Low? Rarity? Mass market? Competitive?

- Packaging – Design? Colour? Quality? Waste?

- Placement – Type of store? Online? Direct sales? Retail? Wholesale?

- Promotion – Advertising? Medium? Web? Seminars? Sales?

The correct mix of each element for your product is critical to marketing success. A high quality brand-name dress selling for $5,000 (product and price) will not sell well if you place it for sale in a dis-

The Management Toolbox

count store and advertise it in the daily classifieds (placement and promotion).

The five P's of marketing add up to how you *position* your product in the market place, in relation to other products in the same category. Positioning may start with the product and the price (note again the example of the high quality dress) but then the other elements need to align with the positioning.

Ultimately where you position your product, and what comprises your marketing mix, is dependent on your target market and your operating costs. It is unlikely that dress' target market is people in a low-income demographic. It is also unlikely that it costs the same to produce as a mass-produced nylon dress. Therefore its packaging will need to be designed attractively and not look cheap; its placement needs to be in a store where people in a high-income demographic would shop; and the promotion would need to be exclusive rather than mass media.

Tips on using the Five P's of Marketing:-

- It is important you start with defining the target market for your product, and the costs of producing and marketing the product.

- Adjust the marketing mix to meet the target market and measure the cost.

Implementing and Measuring

The final collection of management tools can be used to implement change, measure performance and control performance.

A number of tools previously described in Analysing Issues and Developing Solutions can also be used for the management of implementation and the measuring of results:-

- Break-even Analysis (page 38)

- Benchmarking (page 32)

- Employee Engagement Surveys (page 41)

- Teamwork Index (page 54)

- Action Plans (page 126)

- Pareto Chart (page 47)

Change Management Process

When you need to implement and manage change.

What is referred to as "change management" is the process of implementing change in an organisation. The implementation of change has to deal with the human element, which is usually resistant to change.

The critical aspect of any change initiative is therefore to obtain buy-in. Therefore the implementation of change needs to be "managed" in a process that involves identifying the change required, communicating the reasons for the change required and how it will be implemented, carrying out any necessary training, showing the benefits accruing as a result of the proposed change, implementing and evaluating the change.

In his book *Leading Change*, Professor John Kotter provides an eight step process:-

1. Create a sense of urgency – create a significant improvement opportunity to excite people about the need to change;

2. Build a guiding coalition – assemble a group with enough authority and motivation to support and lead a collaborative effort;

3. Create an enticing vision – create a powerful vision of what the world can be like after change, and the benefits it will

bring to everyone, and create a strategy to achieve the vision;

4. Communicate the vision – take every opportunity to explain the vision and the benefits it brings, and in doing so recruit more and more people who are ready and willing to embrace change;

5. Remove obstacles – create structures and systems to support the change, removing any barriers like old systems and structures;

6. Create short term wins – seek and create sure-fire projects that will show how the change is beneficial, track, evaluate and celebrate this stream of small achievements;

7. Build on the change – real change runs deep so don't declare victory too early, continue developing new systems to support the change, find new projects and sustain the momentum;

8. Anchor the change in culture – continue efforts to see that the change is seen in every aspect of the organisation - create new awards and policies and build the new ways of "how we do it here".

Tips on Change Management:-

- Buy a copy of *Leading Change* (John Kotter, Harvard Business Review Press) – a highly readable book on the 8 step process!

The Management Toolbox

Negotiating Using Interests not Positions

When you need to negotiate all interests toward a workable solution.

Whether you are negotiating a sale or a purchase, or negotiating with staff to implement changes, all negotiation should result in the "win-win" solution. The Genghis Khan method of negotiation where one side wins and the other is laid waste is usually not sustainable in business with long term aspirations.

Life is far easier when people have the sense to see things our way. In the real world, however, capital planning, corporate borrowing, annual budgeting, and priority setting all tend to require that people from different organisations - or even our own people with different points of view - find satisfactory means to reach agreement.

For many decision-makers, annual obligations like business plan reviews and budget approvals tend to coincide with increased levels of stress and anxiety. We are well-prepared for the substance to be decided; it's the process that is so unsettling. It can be troublesome if the short-term objective of minimising conflict gets in the way of developing and achieving long-range goals. Interest-based negotiation techniques can help us focus our energy on the process and guide that process towards yielding a satisfactory result.

Most negotiations are repeat performances. We tend to deal with the same bankers, suppliers, clients, directors, managers, etc., for a long time. It is important to recognise and give proper weight to the context in which a negotiation is taking place; if it is within an on-going relationship, the significance of that relationship must be considered.

The Interests Not Positions (INP) model of negotiations seeks to understand the other party's interests, not their stated or assumed positions.

Why focus on Interests, not Positions?

Since most negotiations are with a particular "group" of people, it is human nature to characterise what these "other groups" represent: they are "greedy" or "unhelpful"; they "represent the bank" or "they play to win".

In themselves, these characterisations are not catastrophic in any negotiation, but they do cloak the other person in a "position" that you need to argue against. What happens then is that negotiations follow a path of being "against" a position. For example, in negotiating against a "greedy" person the preparation is based around what you can keep away from them. Where the other side "wants to win" negotiations develop a competitive streak.

Clearly, while someone may have a position (e.g. "I must have a budget increase") they also have an interest behind that position ("I need the budget increase because I am about to launch a new product").

The Management Toolbox

The INP Model is based around moving away from the Position to understand the Interest. Once we know in the above example that they need a budget increase because they are to launch a new product, negotiation can be based around discussions such as risk and return and value for money rather than a quantum increase in the budget.

There may be more than one way of skinning a cat.

The INP Model of negotiation is based on six steps.

1 Separate the people from the situation

Religion teaches us to hate the sin not the sinner. If we view the problem as that which needs to be resolved rather than viewing someone holding a contrary viewpoint as a person to be defeated, the odds of a successful collaboration increase.

One specific technique that can work is to change the shape of the table rather than sitting opposite your 'opponents'. Arrange the seating so that all the parties are sitting together facing a flip chart or blackboard where the problem is presented. That makes it clear that all the participants are facing the problem together, that instead of being "us" against "them", it is a case of "all of us" against "it".

2 Distinguish between Interests and Positions

The classic story to illustrate this describes two sisters fighting over the only orange in the family larder. Each sister must have the entire orange for herself, any less is impossible. A wise parent asks each of the girls (in private) why she wants the orange. One explains she wants to drink the juice; the other wants to use the rind to cook a pudding.

What each sister *wants* is her position, *why* she wants it is her interest. In this case, the simple solution is to give the cook the rind after the juice has been squeezed for the thirsty sister - thus meeting the interests of both.

When preparing for a negotiation, don't just ask "What do they want?" It is also important to ask, "Why do they want it?"

It is equally important - and often more difficult - to ask the same questions about your own views. Many successful negotiators find they will be more successful if they focus on understanding their own interests as they enter discussions.

If they stop themselves from starting out with a pre-determined perfect package, the ideas of others may actually improve their final result.

Negotiators who arrive with a pre-determined package can create real problems. Modifications to their ideas might be taken personally, they may be stubborn, and reaching a satisfactory resolution is made more difficult.

3 Consider your Best Alternative To a Negotiated Settlement or "BATNA"

If you do not reach an agreement with the other, does that really make things worse for you?

If you are negotiating to sell your car and receive an offer $1,000 under your asking price, what is your BATNA? You can refuse to sell it and wait for another offer or you can sell it to the next highest bidder who has agreed you can keep the leather car seat covers from it. The answer depends on your interests and why you wanted to sell the car in the first place. If your interest is to sell the car to pay off your loan, then you have no use of the car seat covers and it may be your BATNA to accept an offer $1,000 under the asking price.

There's an old country & western song about playing poker that summarises the concept of BATNA: "You have to know when to hold and know when to fold." If you know and accept your BATNA, you know when you can simply turn your back on the negotiations. But it is important not to ignore the other party's BATNA. The relative strength of each party's BATNA will determine the balance of power each can exercise, and therefore the compromise that is workable.

4 Remember that silence is golden

This is true for two reasons: If one party is highly opinionated or emotional, if their approach is threatening or extremely demanding, keeping quiet after they finish speaking can be quite unsettling to them. It is like kung-fu; you allow them to be tripped up by their own forcefulness.

Most people are troubled by silence in the midst of heated discussion. Sometimes silence is viewed as disapproval -- but since no specific disapproval has been voiced, it cannot be treated as an attack. It has happened on many occasions that, when met with silence, people have modified their previous statements to make them more palatable, just to bridge their own discomfort at the silence.

Silence is an important element in the crucial tool called Active Listening. The job of a good negotiator is to listen to and understand what others are saying. After all, you can't make an intelligent response to an opinion you do not understand. The discipline of Active Listening requires that you focus on what another person is saying; don't spend your time shaping a stinging response that will put them in their place, no matter how witty and tempting!

Active Listening has some interesting consequences: The listener may actually be able to get a clearer picture of the other party's ideas. And when the listener's response shows just how good a job he or she has done listening, it can shock the other party: "Good grief, they actually paid attention to me!"

One other terrific result of Active Listening is that the discipline of focusing on other opinions can also give the listener the chance to reflect on the process and strategy. Stepping aside and taking a dispassionate view of the goings-on can make one a far more effective negotiator.

5 Pursue fairness

If all the participants view the process as fair, they are more likely to take it seriously and buy into the result. Moreover, the focus on fairness can have an important impact on the substantive result. If the parties to a negotiation can agree on standards against which elements of the agreement can be measured, it can give each a face-saving reason for agreeing. For example, referring to a third-party table of interest rates in a finance negotiation can validate the agreement the parties reach.

The Management Toolbox

To be considered successful, an agreement must be durable. Parties who walk away from the table grumbling may regret their commitment and only honour it grudgingly. If they end up looking for excuses to get out from under an unwanted result, the gains achieved by the other side may prove to be short-term indeed.

6 Only one person can get angry at a time

This is yet another means to help individuals keep a cool head and pay attention to the process and the strategy, as well as the substance of the negotiation. If it's not your "turn" to be angry, the exercise of restraint can be turned into a positive opportunity to observe what is going on with a clear eye. No less important, yelling at each other is not negotiation; it is confrontation. In those situations there may possibly be a 'winner'; but it is even more likely there will be a 'loser'.

In times past, when two property owners had a disagreement, they would hire knights and wage war to reach a conclusion. Then somebody invented lawyers, and the problem-solving process became one of waging law. Our society has reached a level of sophistication in which we recognise that the costs of waging war - or waging law - are terribly high. With the use of good negotiation skills, we have the capacity to reach conclusions in a more satisfactory manner: we can wage PEACE.

Tips on using the Interests Not Positions model:-

- You only get better with practice, so practice the model in all situations

- Prepare before a negotiation – run through the 6 steps in your mind and make sure that you are mentally prepared to be removed from personal feelings and emotions about the negotiation

- During negotiations, consciously ask, "what is the Interest represented by the statements of Position?"

The Management Toolbox

Risk Management Analysis

When you need to identify risks, analyse their effect on the business or project, and prepare plans to mitigate risk.

Risk Management Analysis is a process of identifying risks, assessing risks and developing a strategy to manage risks.

The process involves three steps.

The first step is to identify risks associated with the situation, being the operation of the business, a specific project, or some new idea to be implemented.

It may be useful to first ask what threats exist or may be possible, and then identify the risks to the situation represented by those threats. When you do this, think of the processes and procedures you use in your operations and identify existing and potential risks to any of these.

Risks can come from many sources, so also consider any risks that might arise from:-

- The human element, such as injury or loss of key individuals;

- Reputational incidents such as loss of market confidence or poor employee relationships;

- Natural sources – cyclones, bad weather, natural disasters;

- Political causes like changes in legislation or tax;

- Physical elements like dangerous chemicals, old buildings;

- Operational exposure – failure in third party services like delivery, loss of key suppliers;

- Procedural causes – internal controls being breached, poor supervision, systems failures;

- Financial threats like stock market fluctuations, interest rate changes, fraud;

- Technological sources like new technology, early adoption before testing is complete, technical redundancy;

- Project specific causes – over-budget, over time, inability to achieve required standards.

The second step is to assess the identified risks to arrive at a hierarchy or risks.

This step looks at each identified risk and assesses both the likelihood and the impact of the risk occurring.

The assessment of likelihood can be simply measured on a scale of 1 to 5 where:-

1 = Unlikely

2 = Low likelihood

The Management Toolbox

3 = Medium likelihood

4 = High likelihood

5 = Almost certainly likely

The assessment of impact can also be measured on a scale of 1 to 5:-

1 = Minor impact (limited impact, hardly noticeable)

2 = Low impact (there will be some impact but any impact is manageable by normal means)

3 = Medium impact (impact will be felt and cause concern)

4 = High impact (impact will severely affect normal business)

5 = Catastrophic impact (impact may even cause the business or project to shut down)

Once the likelihood and impact of the risk occurring has been assessed, the risk value can be calculated by multiplying the likelihood score by the impact score and compared with the risk value of all the other risks.

For example, say a business has assessed several risks as follows:-

Risk	Likelihood score	Impact Score	Risk Value Likelihood X Impact
Loss of key manager	3	4	12
Interest rates rise above 5%	2	2	4
Older machines break down	5	3	15

The above example shows that the hierarchy of risks is:-

1. Older machines breaking down
2. Losing a key manager
3. Interest rates rising above 5%

The third step is to then formulate strategies to manage risk before they happen.

In the above example the strategies may be to:-

1. Implement a strict service schedule for the older machines and plan to replace them within 1 year;

2. Insure against the loss of the manager assuming premiums meet a cost-benefit analysis against the effect of that loss;

3. Monitor the interest rate regularly.

Tips on Risk Management Analysis:-

- When you think you have identified all the risks, it is useful to involve others who may have different perspectives, such as customers, other team members, and so on, and ask them what risks they perceive in the context.

- The 1 to 5 scores of likelihood and impact of the risk occurring is quantitative, but assessing the score is qualitative – recognise that but try to assess all risks in the same way. Ultimately the Risk Value is only a way of achieving a hierarchy of risk and is not meant to be a definitive measure of the value of the risk.

- Once you have formulated strategies, complete the plan by nominating who is responsible for the implementation of the strategy, when by (dictated by the seriousness of the risk) and how often it should be monitored.

Experiential Transfer Process

When you need to transfer conceptual training to day to day activity.

The Experiential Transfer Process is based on training outcomes that show that different ways of delivering training produces different rates of retention.

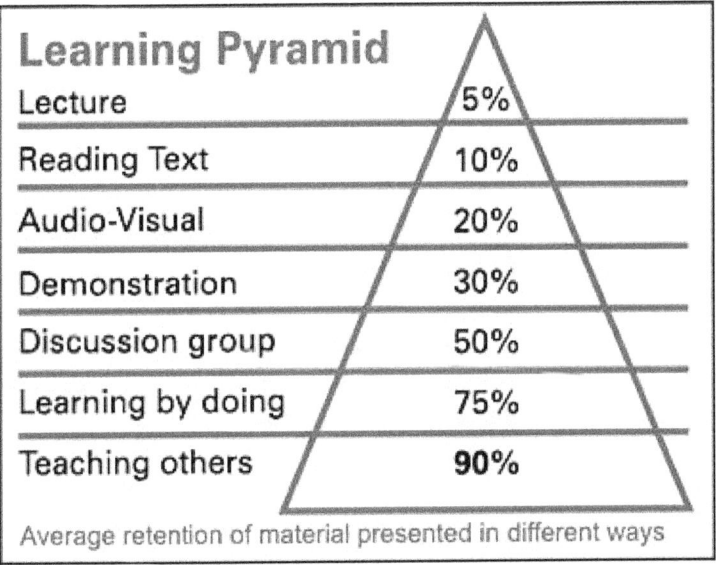

The above Learning Pyramid was developed by National Training Laboratories, Bethel, Maine.

It shows the average rates of retention of training material presented in different ways. You retain the least information from simply attending a lecture, and progressively retain more as you progress down the pyramid, retaining the most when you teach others.

As you manage training in your company, in order to ensure that your team members retain as much learning from the training as possible, you need to focus on presenting the training using the passive methods from lectures with reading texts and audio-visual presentations, and then combine those methods with demonstrations, discussion and practice.

After the passive training methods, you can start to provide participatory training by practicing what has been taught and holding discussions afterwards, based around the experience of putting the learning into practice and asking three questions:-

1. What happened? Having learned the lesson and experienced it through some practice, discuss what people learned and felt as they practiced the learning;

2. So what? Having discussed what people observed during the practice, discuss what can be learned from those experiences and how it relates to the workplace.

3. Now what? Finally discuss what should be done with what has been learned, arriving at some plans on implementation.

Tips for using the Experiential Transfer Process:-

- Plan all training with a mixture of presentation methods

- Actively include an opportunity for trainees to use the learning and learn by doing – this forms the basis of the experience to be discussed over the three questions

- As soon as possible after the training, allow trainees to teach someone else

The Management Toolbox

Ratio Analysis

When you need to measure your financial performance against past periods, against others, or against industry averages.

"Ratio Analysis" is a quantitative analysis of information found in your financial reports. They describe relationships between different numbers and understanding them allows you to measure financial performance.

Financial ratios allow you to compare different aspects of your financial performance against past periods to see if you have improved or not, against competitors to see how you compare, and against industry averages to identify room for improvement.

Financial ratios can measure your liquidity and solvency, efficiency, profitability, and financial leverage. Here are some key ratios:-

- Current Ratio = Current Assets divided by Current Liabilities and expressed as a ratio. For example, Current Assets of $200,000 against Current Liabilities of $180,000 is expressed as a Current Ratio of $1.1:$1 or "for every $1 of Current Liability, there is $1.10 to cover". This is a measure of liquidity – the higher the ratio the better, the minimum "safe" ratio being 1:1.

- Quick Ratio = Cash, cash equivalents, assets quickly convertible to cash divided by Current Liabilities. This is also called the "Acid Test Ratio" and measures liquidity or the level of cash assets to Current Liabilities and answers the question, "How much of my Current Liabilities can I pay right now?" Again the higher the ratio the better, for example a ratio of 2:1 means that for every dollar of current liability you have $2 in cash or assets quickly convertible to cash. A negative ratio is cause for concern.

- Accounts Receivable Turnover = Sales divided by Average Accounts Receivable. This measures efficiency – how many times can a business turn accounts receivable into cash during a period. For example annual Sales of $1,000,000 divided by average balance of Accounts Receivable in a year of $150,000 is a turnover of 6.7 times. This means that this business converts accounts receivable to cash 6.7 times a year. You can use this to calculate how long it takes to convert accounts receivables by dividing the number of months by 6.7 i.e. it takes 1.8 months to collect from a sale. You can use this information to try to increase efficiency by reducing the collection period.

- Inventory Turnover = Purchases divided by Average Inventory value. This is another efficiency ratio and measures how quickly your inventory turns over. Annual Purchases of $800,000 against Inventory levels of $200,000 means a turn of 4 times a year – on average stock sits on your shelves for about (12/4) 3 months before it is sold.

- Gross Profit Ratio = Gross Profit divided by Sales. This is a profitability measure and measures how much gross profit you make per sale. If Gross Profit (after direct cost of goods but before overhead expenses) were $100,000 and Sales were $600,000, the Gross Profit Ratio is 16.7%, or, for every dollar sale you make profit before overheads of 16.7 cents.

- Return on Investment = Net Profit divided by Cost of Investment. This ratio measures profitability and tells you what returns you are getting for each dollar invested. "Net Profit" can be before tax, before interest and tax, or after all taxes and interest – just make sure you are comparing like for like. The Cost of Investment can sometimes be substituted with the Cost of Capital Employed. For example the net assets used in the business (plant & equipment, cash and investments, less liabilities) might be $1,000,000. If Net Profit for the year were $200,000 then the Return on Investment is calculated as 200,000/1,000,000 or 20%. You can then asses this against bank interest and assess whether your business returns sufficiently for the risk premium attached.

Tips on using Ratio Analysis:-

1. Compare like to like, for example don't use Net Profit this year *before* tax in a ratio, and compare it against the previous year's Net Profit *after* tax.

2. Ratio Analysis is about trends, not necessarily as a measure in itself. For example if your Quick Ratio was 1:1 this may seem reasonable. However if you compare it to last month when it was 2:1 you would have to be looking at why your solvency has deteriorated.

3. Ratio Analysis is about comparison. For example if in the next month your Quick Ratio returned to it's long term average of 2:1 you might be pleased, until you compare it to industry averages and find that for your industry the average is 3:1.

The Balanced Scorecard

When you need to quantify your vision and measure performance.

The Balanced Scorecard is a tool for strategic management of an organisation created by Robert S Kaplan and David P Norton. Readers of this Toolbox are recommended to read their book *The Balanced Scorecard: Translating Strategy Into Action* (1996, Harvard Business School Press).

The Balanced Scorecard is based on the premise that long term Vision and Strategy is linked to short term operational control, and the relationship can be viewed from four vital perspectives of the long term:-

1. The Customer Perspective

2. The Financial Perspective

3. The Internal Process Perspective

4. The Learning and Growth Perspective

Once the long term Vision is described in this way, it creates a performance framework of key measures that control the drive towards the long term objectives.

The four perspectives are arrived at by asking the questions:-

1. To achieve our Vision, how should we look to our customers?
2. To achieve our Vision, how should our finances look?
3. To achieve our Vision what key business processes must we excel at?
4. To achieve our Vision how do we sustain our ability to learn and grow?

In answering these questions you quantify what it means to have achieved the Vision. For example the first question may identify the following:-

To achieve our Vision we should look like the following to our customers:-

- *Responsive service*
- *Experts in our field*
- *Value for Money*

These values can then be quantified to describe what "success" in each value means, for example:-

- *Responsive service means that we reply to customer queries within 24 hours*
- *Expertise means that we satisfy 90% of all technical queries within the responsive timeframes*

The Management Toolbox

- *Value for money means customers prefer our products against our competitors 70% of the time*

Key measurements can then be defined and measured such as:-

- *Number of customer queries still open after 24 hours*

- *Number of technical queries not satisfied within 24 hours*

- *Annual customer survey showing their attitude to our value for money*

The Balanced Scorecard methodology can then be used to create a "dashboard" of key measures and ratios as a strategic summary of performance.

Tips on using the Balanced Scorecard:-

- You can purchase a copy of Kaplan & Norton's original paper *Using the Balanced Scorecard as a Strategic Management System* from the Harvard Business Review website

- Understand your Vision first – what is it that means "success" in your business?

- Remember to create a dashboard of *key* measurements – too many can be distracting

Tools in Alphabetical Order

Action Planning 126
Affinity Diagram 91
The Balanced Scorecard 158
Benchmarking 32
Brainstorming 21
Break-even Analysis 38
Business Model Canvas 101
Business Planning 121
Cause & Effect Diagram 63
Change Management Process 136
Check Sheet 30
Critical Path Analysis 128
Crossover Analysis 94
Customer Attractiveness Index 88
Customer Value Matrix 74
Decision Tree 78
Employee Engagement Survey 41
Experiential Transfer Process 151
Five P's of Marketing 133
Five Why's 66
Flowchart 28
Force Field Analysis 112
Job Descriptions 107
LACE 14
Management Presentation 99
Market Segmentation 36
Mind Mapping 25

Negotiating Using Interests not Positions ... 138
Nominal Group Technique ... 23
Organisation Charts ... 105
Pareto Chart ... 47
The Pareto Principle ... 77
PESTLE ... 43
Pie Chart ... 49
Policies and Procedures ... 109
The Problem-Solving Model ... 5
The Product Development Process ... 82
Product Features and Benefits Analysis ... 72
Quality Circles ... 103
Ratio Analysis ... 154
Risk Management Analysis ... 146
Run Chart ... 34
Sales Component Analysis ... 130
Scatter Diagram ... 68
Scenario Analysis ... 124
Six Thinking Hats ... 10
SMART ... 17
Strategic Planning ... 118
Stratification ... 61
SWOT Analysis ... 45
Teamwork Index ... 54
Training Matrix ... 97
Urgent/Important Matrix ... 51
Venn Diagram ... 70
Vision and Mission Statements ... 115

Tools by Task

Task	Tools
To decide which problem will be addressed first (or next)	Flow chart (page 28) Check sheet (page 30) Pareto chart (page 47) Brainstorming (page 21) Nominal Group Technique (page 23) Urgent/Important Matrix (page 51) Flowchart (page 28) Six Thinking hats (page 10) LACE (page 14)
To arrive at a statement that describes the problem in terms of what it is specifically, where it occurs, when it happens, and its extent	Check sheet (page 30) Pareto chart (page 47) Run chart (page 34) Pie chart (page 49) Venn Diagram (page 70) Stratification (page 61) Flowchart (page 28) Six Thinking Hats (page 10) SMART (page 17)
To develop a complete picture of all the possible cause(s) of the problem	Check sheet (page 30) Venn Diagram (page 70) Affinity Diagram (page 91) Cause and effect diagram (page 63) Brainstorming (page 21) Five Why's (page 66) Mind Mapping (page 25)

The Management Toolbox

To agree on the basic cause(s) of the problem	Flowchart (page 28) Problem-Solving Model (page 5) Six Thinking Hats (page 10) Check sheet (page 30) Pareto chart (page 47) Scatter diagram (page 68) Brainstorming (page 21) Nominal Group Technique (page 23) Five Why's (page 66) Six Thinking Hats (page 10) LACE (page 14)
To develop an effective and implementable solution and action plan	Brainstorming (page 21) Force Field analysis (page 112) Management presentation (page 99) Pie chart (page 49) Affinity Diagram (page 91) Benchmarking (page 32) Flowchart (page 28) Problem-Solving Model (page 5) Six Thinking Hats (page 10) LACE (page 14) Action Planning (page 126) Critical Path Analysis (page 128) SMART (page 17)
To implement the solution and establish needed monitoring procedures and charts	Pareto chart (page 47) Stratification (page 61) Benchmarking (page 32) Quality Circles (page 103) Affinity Diagram (page 91)

To plan and organize within the business	Problem-Solving Model (page 5) Action Planning (page 126) SMART (page 17) Vision and Mission statements (page 115) Strategic Planning (page 118) Business planning (page 121) PESTLE (page 43) SWOT Analysis (page 45) The Balanced Scorecard (page 158) Action Planning (page 126) Management Presentation (page 99) Business Model Canvas (page 101) Scenario analysis (page 124) Market segmentation (page 36) SMART (page 17)
To plan marketing and sales	Market segmentation (page 36) Product Features and Benefits (page 72) SWOT Analysis (page 45) Customer Value Matrix (page 74) Customer Attractiveness Matrix (page 88) Sales component analysis (page 130) Five P's of Marketing (page 133) Action Planning (page 126)

The Management Toolbox

To choose between different options	SMART (page 17) Decision Tree (page 78) Affinity Diagram (page 91) The Pareto Principle (page 77) Break-even Analysis (page 38) Crossover Analysis (page 94) SWOT Analysis (page 45) Nominal Group Technique (page 23)
To create teamwork and organize workforce effectively	Training Matrix (page 97) Organisation Charts (page 105) Venn Diagram (page 70) Job descriptions (page 107) Policies and procedures (page 109) Experiential Transfer Process (page 151) Negotiating using Interests not Positions (page 138) Nominal Group Technique (page 23) Teamwork Index (page 54) Employee Engagement Survey (page 41) LACE (page 14) Quality Circles (page 103)
To plan for and manage risk	Scenario analysis (page 124) Risk Management Analysis (page 146) SWOT Analysis (page 45)
To manage the finances	Ratio Analysis (page 154)

	Break-even Analysis (page 38) Crossover Analysis (page 94) Sales Component Analysis (page 130)
To manage change	Change Management Process (page 136) Experiential Transfer Process (page 151) Quality Circles (page 103) The Balanced Scorecard (page 158) Critical Path Analysis (page 128) Negotiating using Interests not Positions (page 138) Six Thinking Hats (page 10) LACE (page 14)
To manage the introduction of new products	The Product Development Process (page 82) SWOT Analysis (page 45) Quality Circles (page 103)

The Management Toolbox

www.ingramcontent.com/pod-product-compliance
Lightning Source LLC
Chambersburg PA
CBHW060848170526
45158CB00001B/277